THE MIGHTY GASTROPOLIS: PORTLAND

THE MIGHTY GASTROPOLIS
PORTLAND

A JOURNEY THROUGH THE CENTER OF AMERICA'S NEW FOOD REVOLUTION

Karen Brooks with Gideon Bosker and Teri Gelber

Photographs by Gideon Bosker and Karen Brooks

CHRONICLE BOOKS

SAN FRANCISCO

Portions of pieces on Gabriel Rucker, Kevin Gibson, Boke Bowl, and Din Din Supper Club have been reprinted from *Portland Monthly* magazine with permission.

Library of Congress Cataloging-in-Publication Data available.

ISBN 978-1-4521-0596-3

Manufactured in China

Designed by Alice Chau
Typesetting by DC Typography

10 9 8 7 6 5 4 3 2 1

Chronicle Books LLC
680 Second Street
San Francisco, California 94107
www.chroniclebooks.com

Acknowledgments

It took a village of visionaries, provocateurs, family heroes, daredevil cooks, and outrageously generous friends to bring *The Mighty Gastropolis* to life. My everlasting thanks to:

Gideon Bosker, my longtime collaborator, who brainstormed with me from Day One and animated Portland's food scene through his strange and wonderful photographic vision.

Teri Gelber, cook extraordinaire and my trusted sidekick, for bringing her exacting standards to recipe testing.

The Chronicle Books team, especially our fantastic editor Sarah Billingsley, the all-around wonder woman who championed this project, and Richard Pine, our long-time friend and agent.

My posse at *Portland Monthly* magazine, a deep well of support and inspiration. With love and gratitude to owner Nicole Vogel, irreplaceable editors Randy Gragg and Rachel Ritchie, esteemed comrade Zach Dundas, my best pal and photo assistant Ben Tepler, and the rest of my office family.

Sandy Rowe and the *Oregonian*, for years of journalism support.

The grand pals who scratched through drafts and shared culinary philosophy: Mike Thelin, Thomas Lauderdale, Philip Iosca, Susan Orlean, Billy Galperin, Matt Kramer, Miriam Seger, Robert Reynolds, Shawn Levy, Barry Johnson, Martha Holmberg, Carrie Welch, Trink Morimitsu, DK Holm, and Lena Lencek. Peter Leitner, ally, "brother," the catalyst for this project, thank you!

To stellar friends and master cheerleaders: Victoria Frey, Julien Leitner, Joan Strouse, Rabbi Gary Schoenberg, Shirley Kishiyama, Edward Taub, Tracy and Dan Oseran, Paul and Lauren Schneider, Susan Hoffman, Josie Mosely, Marty Hughley, Jeff Conti, Paige Powell, Joe Soprani, Iris Wolf, Carol Conrades, and Michael Sills. Jon Gramsted, you are a prince. Brett, Jodi and Gavin Fleishman, I love you. Big thanks to Tanya Supina and Christopher and Theo Gelber. We miss you, Dorka.

Finally, to all the Portland cooks and food creatives who generously shared untold stories and the recipes that changed everything.

For Mom, who doggedly chewed over every word, and my brother, Craig, massive in every way, unrelenting in generosity. From my deepest corners, with love and thanks for always believing in me.

CONTENTS

CHAPTER 4

SUPPER CLUB
RENEGADES

Communal tables are never-ending dinner parties with some of the best food to be found: boisterous, bountiful, and barely legal.

CHAPTER 5

FOOD-CART REBELS

Portland's pavement gourmets create food malls and town squares of the future.

CHAPTER 6

THE NEW PIONEERS

Small-batch coffee roasters, salumi fanatics, and daring entrepreneurs detour away from corporate models to blaze fresh trails.

INTRODUCTION

DISPATCHES FROM THE CULINARY RENEGADE ZONE

Two years before he became the poster boy for Portland's rise to the national food stage, Le Pigeon's Gabriel Rucker struck the scene like a lightning storm. He was twenty-five and a virtual unknown, a fast-rapping hired gun with a flock of tattooed birds swooping up his arm, brought in to reinvent a failing cult restaurant on a forgotten street.

Almost overnight, he defined the playful attitude and affordable artisan cuisine that firmly planted a place called "Stumptown" on the gastronomic map. Rucker's burger set the tone, served with an elegant bistro knife plunged through the heart of its tall-boy bun. Soon, food lovers and discerning critics from the *New York Times* were drooling over other creations: brazen beef cheek bourguignon and foie gras profiteroles, a swaggering plate of foie gras ice cream, foie gras caramel, and foie gras powdered sugar. *Escoffier mon dieu!*

With its nonconformist cooking and punk-rock vibes, Le Pigeon embodies what *Time* magazine's Josh Ozersky calls "America's New Food Eden," a hotbed of locavorism, food-truck living, high/low eating, and animal fever. But Le Pigeon is only the beginning.

Across town, veteran backpacker Andy Ricker is mining his twenty-year journey as a Thai food savant at Pok Pok. The signature charcoal-blasted chicken dish arrives on a bare plate, with a wad of sticky rice sheathed in plastic wrap; real-deal *khao soi kai* noodles—hotter than brimstone fire—exit a take-out window. From afar, this indoor/outdoor village of Cambodian rock music and Asian "drinking foods" looks like outcast cuisine, dining on the fringe. But Ricker's powerful cooking and strange vision, plopped in a front yard on a local speedway, shows just how far obsession and a do-it-yourself mentality can take you: Ricker's humble eatery has been lauded as "America's best Thai restaurant," as followers liken his chicken wings to "crack cocaine." Now Pok Pok has invaded New York, the fooderati are tracking every move, and Ricker is a wing king, indeed.

Portland diners are leaping into action. At St. Jack, a local restaurant collective tucked into a bike-centric neighborhood, the cooking team riffs on France's jolly, offal-loving dens of informality, the *bouchons* of Lyon. Boys with skinny ties shake flirty drinks, Oregon pinot flows like the mighty Columbia, and boisterous plates of fried tripe and blood sausages make the city's porky excesses, in comparison, seem worthy of the surgeon general's blessing. Even stuffed duck necks—served full steam and head on—sell out routinely. Enthuses foodie financier Kurt Huffman: "We had a sense our customers were adventurous, but now it's 'Bring it on!' We can't make stuff weird enough."

This book is a journey through the mighty gastropolis of Portland, Oregon, population of food lovers unknown, but game for almost anything, even when served on hand-me-down dishware. In this willfully eccentric pasture of pleasure, restaurants are good-vibe places that feel more like art projects than conventional eateries. This is where guerrilla gourmets go their own way, transforming "grown in Oregon" foodstuffs into gustatory experiments in spaces often hammered, sawed, and welded by hand. Throughout the city, low-budget storefronts and "pop-up" dining rooms barely hint at what awaits inside: candlelit intimacy, personal playlists, irrepressibly seductive food.

In these egalitarian eating enclaves, it's hard to tell the waiters from the diners, and dishes come on like indie rockers: spare and unpretentious. Communal tables take center stage, as Portland practices its own brand of Bolshevik eating, an elbow-to-elbow, knife-to-knife, come-as-you-are food fest that merrily cuts through the bubble-wrap isolation of haute cuisine. Meanwhile, a grass-roots arsenal of

raised, foraged, distilled, fermented, brewed, butchered, or bartered goods is the baseline for the new gastronomic luxury: 500-thread-count comfort food.

At Boke Bowl, diners hunker down at long, sturdy tables to eat ramen teeming with handcrafted noodles and, yes, fried chicken. Evoe, a house of hyper-local worship, has eaters swooning in the vapors of forest mushrooms fresh from a forager's trunk. Laurelhurst Market sizzles as the country's first alternative steakhouse, with affordable cuts and a rollicking neighborhood vibe. The Big Egg food cart, a street-side temple to fried-egg sandwiches, embodies this new spirit of out-of-home dining: freedom of expression, a one-of-a-kind experience, be-your-own boss on your own terms.

Gone are stagnant menus, ossified ideas about the cooking arts, the tyranny of sameness. Instead of doctrinaire treatises that enshrine culinary perfection, shelves hold dog-eared spiral notebooks with recipes that read like Dada poems or dream books. The inspirations for Portland's food scene are domestic, global, and "whatever." Judging by the two-hour waits for a taste, these culinary ruffians have hit a gustatory nerve.

Portland is a growing vegan stronghold, with cafés, food carts, and a vegan strip club to champion the style. But the uprising hasn't threatened the supremacy of Porkland, with its squealing menus and "no animal left behind" butchery underground. Without a doubt, pork is the new salmon. The meat-curing mad men at Olympic Provisions support a "head salumist," while the Portland Meat Collective leads the charge on continuing education, offering classes such as Pig's Head Butchery and Ladies' Home Pig Butchery. Porklandia, indeed.

What unites them all: Oregon's copious natural resources, the showcase and high point of menus at every level. It doesn't hurt that enterprising pickers and pluckers wheel up to the back doors of restaurants, scales in hand, to peddle wild porcini the size of small purses or twenty kinds of heirloom tomatoes. Or that bustling farmers' markets across the city sell the most glistening, color-saturated produce on the planet—what you'd imagine fruits and vegetables would look like at roadside stands in heaven. Cooks come to Oregon and say they can only dream of such readily available abundance. Remarked A-caliber

chef Eric Ripert of New York's Le Bernadín on one visit: "This is the best place on earth, the end of the rainbow. I envy you."

We've been there from the beginning, chronicling and dissecting every bite. *The Mighty Gastropolis* goes to the core of a food revolution sparked by a new consciousness that reflects the values and ideals of every youthful generation since the 1980s. It shows how a people's army of "outsider" cooks, maverick food carters, supper clubbers, coffee auteurs, and crazed charcuterists rose to create an artisanal and bohemian foodopolis unlike any other place in the country.

In these pages, you'll meet these culinary innovators and plucky entrepreneurs: the natty baristas who took the art of coffee roasting straight to the street; the gentle giant who brings extreme seasonality to bagels while tending his hand-forged wood oven, often in the rain; and chefs like Rucker and Ricker, who have negotiated the journey from culinary obscurity to James Beard awards and Food Network shout-outs.

Consider the story of wilderness stalker-cum-modernist thinker Matt Lightner, who blazed a new Oregon trail that left "farm to table" in the dust. With techniques gleaned from top foodie think tanks in Copenhagen and Spain, the twenty-eight-year-old foraged the state's forests and streams for hidden larder and a fresh definition of local cooking. He put mysterious botanicals and architecturally constructed dishes in a reserved restaurant known for great steak *frites*, Castagna in Southeast Portland. While some chefs make menus out of whole animals from nose to tail, Lightner considers what the beast eats and where it plays, then harnesses the taste of clover, the smoke of hay, and, sometimes, it seems, even the good long nap the beast might take under a white oak, all of it becoming a culinary ecosystem on the plate. Each plate tells a story with edible characters sniffed out on riverbanks, swept off the forest floor, or nurtured in vegetable beds planted next door in the front yard of the True Value Hardware store. New York spirited him away to open a seventeen-seat dream restaurant, but he willed to Portland an original modernist cuisine.

We also extracted our favorite recipes from the movement's reluctant heroes and gastro-generals, among them meat temptress Naomi Pomeroy and chocolate explorer

David Briggs, whose exquisite Raleigh Bars are the thinking person's Snickers: one bite, and there's no going back. It takes only heart and guts to replicate the crush-worthy dishes stoking Portland's embers: Navarre's halibut emerging from the oven under a "soufflé" of garlic aïoli; Pok Pok's grilled corn, formulated with an outrageous soak of salty coconut cream; and, of course, Tastebud's raw asparagus and whole lemon "pesto," a pure taste of tart, grassy, wild deliciousness.

You will find instructions for baked apples the Portland way—for breakfast, with bacon lardons and spiced maple syrup, á la Tasty n Sons—and barbecue sauce as only Le Pigeon could imagine it: with Chinese mustard, oranges, prune juice, and, yes, a couple of bobbing bird heads if you're so inclined. We even unlocked the secrets to the best cupcakes ever: with caramel-dripping potato chips planted like conqueror's flags in the elegant ganache frosting, courtesy of the Sugar Cube food cart.

Sitting at these tables, eating this food, you can't help but taste something new: a cuisine of the mulch, a dreamscape of meat galore and miraculous potatoes, and of reinvented marshmallows, pressed into service for those who want their food to taste like it's still connected to the land. Whether they practice their craft from the hot plate of a food cart or a stepped-up professional kitchen, Portland's best chefs, like other dedicated artists, are jazzed about exploring the possibilities that ingredients—in their incalculable combinations—have for producing experiences.

So how did a ruggedly handsome city with the hokey nickname Stumptown—a place where you might encounter 7,000 nude bike riders on your way to brunch—become the great new American food city?

First, given low barriers to entry and loose regulations, brave entrepreneurs can attain small dreams here. Rents are cheaper than those in most cities, enabling cooks at all levels to take risks in low-cost digs, on their own terms. Liquor licenses cost $500, among the cheapest in the United States. In most cities, a start-up of a quarter of a million dollars is more like it, shutting the door for independents. In Portland, even a food cart can specialize in handmade beer. Meanwhile, wine-buying rules in most other markets favor deep pockets, bulk purchases, and "incentive" buying. In cash-state Oregon, restaurants can buy what they want, be it one case or a measly

bottle; everyone pays the same, allowing a quirky storefront to geek out on rosés or eighty different wines by the glass. Wheeling and dealing in Portland means negotiating for a small-batch local whiskey or prying a stash of wild morels from a forager.

Second, access to prime ingredients is unrivaled. The city's progressive urban-growth-boundary laws insure that farms flourish inside and outside the city limits. Nowhere in America—and, increasingly, rarely in Europe—can chefs get as close to the lush spawning grounds of fruits, berries, wine grapes, fish, organic meats, and other ingredients that underpin Portland's restaurant culture. Meanwhile, you can't throw a crumbled eco-napkin without striking an artisanal producer of one kind or another. These small-batch coffee roasters, bakers, charcuterists, distillers, and dairy farmers are the bone and marrow of an extreme "think local" food movement. At the same time, the entire citizenry is seemingly engaged in urban farming, cheese making, beekeeping, and food bartering, while obsessing over local restaurants via Twitter alerts.

On Saturday, the engine room of Portland's food laboratory hums in a downtown park lined with old elm trees: the Portland Farmers' Market, one of the most remarkable farm-to-city shopping centers in America, unique in every dimension of bird, bread, and greens. This is the city's food armory and the epicenter of Portland's vast market scene. Here, in a microcosm of the mighty gastropolis, uncorrupted ingredients and their handmade offspring pour in at unprecedented rates. Vendors treat vegetables like art stars, each booth a personalized exhibit. Installations of cauliflowers in rainbow hues stand next to haystacks of wonderful oddball mushrooms straight from Oregon's spooky woods, and, everywhere, boxes and boxes of glimmering berries.

Oregon grows the finest strawberries to be found, plus most of the world's black raspberries, the second-largest blackberry crop, and nearly all of the planet's mysteriously delicious marionberries. And that doesn't count the rows and rows of stalls housing mad picklers, honey freaks, and serious bakers. Meat, of course, is everywhere, a stampede of heritage turkeys, yak, buffalo, "free-browse" chevon goats, pork parts supreme, and ethically raised beef plumped on the Willamette Valley's fertility. A stall sign sums it up: "Yeh Baby, Elk Steaks Are In." Market mystic Gene Thiel

KNOW YOUR BUTCHER.

PORTLAND, OR

FROSTY'S
• ONE OF A KIND •
• 7 DIFFERENT CHILES •
CHILE FLAKE
IT'S
SMOKIN'
HOT
$3.00
(2 oz

epitomizes the life: one man so deeply connected to his crops that, even in his late seventies, he treks 300 miles every weekend to stand at his booth all day, because he loves the idea that we're eating his food. You don't have to ask if these unscrubbed purple carrots, with wild white stripes through their cores, are "organic."

In large food cities, pedigreed ingredients are normally reserved for the restaurant elite. In Portland, even good sandwich shops receive "house calls" from quality growers often known only by nicknames like the Asparaguy. "A million guys are selling wild mushrooms; I was offered eight varieties today, some I'd never heard of," remarks Navarre chef John Taboada, a pioneer of Portland's indie food scene. "On the East Coast these would be insanely priced. Where I came from, in D.C., we'd have to use them in some specific way to extend their value. Here, we grill them like steaks or shave them into raw salads—uses you've never considered before. We talk, buy, experiment. Prices are so reasonable, we can be a little reckless."

As much as anything, the story of *The Mighty Gastropolis* is found in the heart of a city where quality of life trumps most everything. For years, Portland was a backwater, its food scene relegated to the kids' table while rival sister Seattle sat with the big boys. It turned out to be a blessing. Freed from expectations and the media spotlight, cooks invested in ideas, camaraderie, and community. That's the Portland way.

This is a rough-and-tumble place; paradise one day, then soaked in puddles of doom the next. Even a glimmer of bright light can disappear for month-long stretches. Meanwhile, economic growth since World War II has been paltry. And yet everything you could want under the sun is here—affordability, friendly vibes, the great outdoors, and ecstatic eating around every corner—except for the sun itself and money. In Portland, you have to create your own shot, make your own sunshine. The simple fact is this: People are here because they want to be here. We've grown a culture of intentionality—small-scale, proudly quirky, and open to anything, as long as it's good. Damned few are getting rich, yet living well is considered a birthright.

Instead of statement architecture and tourist monuments, Portland believes in unsexy things: mass transit, civic pride, and a vibrant downtown ten minutes away from an urban forest reserve, one of the country's largest, marked by brooding old-growth fir, running trails, and a perennial chaos of green. It also believes everyone is entitled to a great meal. It is mind-set as much as cuisine: taking simple things and making them incredible without being yoked to the bottom line. In the end, rolodexes don't matter in Stumptown; the meal card is judged by commitment and originality. If you're financially successful, great, but it's not the litmus test.

Food festival impresario Mike Thelin, cofounder of Feast Portland, hits on a central point: "There's something special about this culture. If you embrace it, it will open up, take you in, wrap its arms around you. But try to do something that doesn't fit, and it will reject you like a bad kidney."

Camaraderie lies at the heart of Portland's food nation. The long list of farms and other providers posted on restaurant walls and menus announces that you're in an interconnected community of food connoisseurs, where showcasing each other's salumi and craft liquors is a given. Unlike the petty, cutthroat world of the big city, where competitive secrets are tightly held, Portland's "Che gourmets" are quick to blurt out, "Dude, do you want to know my secret lamb source?" It's a tight-knit group and more generous than the Red Cross, ceaselessly throwing benefits for wounded soldiers with decommissioned kitchens, or donating their sweat and blood sausages to nonprofits and disaster-torn countries.

Portland is now an ongoing party host. The food-show cameras, *New York Times* reporters, James Beard judges, glossy magazine critics, and food-loving tourists are regular guests, as familiar in the backdrop as eco-plates and recycling bins. Why? Perhaps they've all been touched by what is finally unique about this pirate food network: These cooks are in it for all the right reasons, creating a culture of possibility and letting it unfold organically. In a world where trust and authenticity are in short supply, they remind us of what we're seeking: a noncorporate, affordable, creative, globally aware, and, above all, genuine expression of life. From the moment you walk in the door, you feel at home, and part of something larger. This doesn't exist any place else.

All of this helps explain why, in money-strapped times, Portland has evolved the country's most talked-about food cart scene, where, in dedicated block-long clusters, next-generation food entrepreneurs band together in personalized shacks, selling things not typical of vendors anywhere else: wood-oven pizzas; foie gras and chips; sandwiches on cart-baked bread with fresh-smoked ham; or extravagant chocolate cupcakes garnished with potato chips and a bath of caramel sauce—all served (relatively) inexpensively with a side of attitude. These "food-cart communities," like the traveling circuses and sideshows of days past, exemplify how talent at the margins can coalesce into sybaritic sweet zones that attract all comers. The young and broke are eating it up, but so are foodies, food critics, and office workers.

There is a political dialectic in Portland's great food cart experiment, now 600 carts strong and growing. Perhaps no other "job market" in America signals the struggles of the time so vividly. But, here, chefs and wannabe chefs, flush with bright ideas, capture what the October 24, 2011, *New York* magazine called the "Sucks to be Us" generation, the "Wake up, you have no idea, please don't fire me" youthful hordes looking for a way to come of age and find their way out of the cul-de-sacs of "post-hope America."

The food carts open avenues to encourage and test the small-business, entrepreneurial spirit that forms the titanium backbone of economic vitality. They embark on this risk-to-reward journey with unprecedented spunk, ingenuity, and idealism, and for that leap alone, we must love and admire them. And, in galvanizing neighborhoods otherwise lacking brick-and-mortar magnets for social intercourse, they promote connectivity in real time, a form of human gathering that seems to be in short supply. In their world, food married to artisanal excellence is their best hope for a meal ticket—and a community's best shot at making streets sing with human chatter and conviviality. Portland's cart smarts may be the way of the future.

Portland's casual gastronomy can be traced all the way back to Michael Vidor, a sly-smiling, pot-smoking, Harvard-educated restaurateur who dressed like a homeless person while running L'Auberge and Genoa, legendary high-end spots in Portland's grittiest locations. Vidor could recite every boxing champ in history, but he didn't have a clue when it came to cooking. No matter. He knew what he liked, and with no experience, he conceptualized "fine" dining in Portland: no fussy food, no pretension, no throwing dishes. In 1969, L'Auberge, a tumbledown storefront on West Burnside, stood as Portland's first low-rent "don't call us

French" haute-cuisine restaurant, a model handed down for future generations. Among his radical ideas: the kitchen as collegial laboratory far removed from the Orwellian hellholes of *Down and Out in Paris and London.*

Still, for many years, Portland was largely a culinary wasteland, where you closed your eyes and pulled Lender's bagels from Safeway's deep freeze. But maverick models always surfaced, including what was surely the world's first microeatery, Briggs and Crampton, with one table, onesitting, one meal a day—lunch—for two people only. It took six months to snag a reservation. Take *that*, Momofuku Ko.

In a state with no regional cuisine, no defining dishes, no take-to-the-grave secrets, the cult of ingredients has always reigned. For years, fennel sprouted from sidewalk cracks, salmon and sturgeon—*sturgeon!*—jumped freely in the rivers, and local produce, what native son James Beard called "the round of the earth's gifts to the palate," sold at a pittance to anyone with a U-Pick bucket. Times changed when Greg Higgins pedaled by bike from New York to Portland, envisioned a farm-to-table future, and recruited like-minded chefs Cory Schreiber (Wildwood) and Vitaly Paley (Paley's Place) to the dream in the 1990s. These spiritual daddies harnessed the state's staggering bounty into a grower-connected model, adding big-city professionalism and setting the stage for Portland's climb as a food-savvy destination.

But tapping local provenance was only the beginning. The generation that followed waged war on America's conformist culture of food to create something of their own, far removed from the white-hot centers of Michelin stars. Like Portland itself, their food world is deliberate and self-possessed. You won't find the next Mugaritz or Per Se here, and it is unlikely that this diversity-challenged city will spawn miniature cities perfumed by ethnic wonders like the Koreatowns and Japantowns of Los Angeles and New York. Portland is something else: a risk-taking, no-rules spawning ground—a grand little test kitchen inspiring even some of the old guard to its ways. This guerrilla food community is an incubator, an oven, if you will, for the kind of creativity that Phil Knight demonstrated when he made his first Nike shoe sole on a griddle iron. After all, Stumptown Coffee Roasters started in a glorified garage; not too long ago, owner Duane Sorensen was just another local dude. Now he's a global kingpin who has changed the coffee conversation. It can happen here.

This is the story of cooks like Tommy Habetz, once an aide-de-camp to Mario Batali, who walked away from the swanky set in New York City to create the place he always wanted. His Bunk Sandwiches serves gutsy flavors, a punk-rock aesthetic, and enough inspiration to land him a slot in *Coco*, a major tome on 100 contemporary food stars. Over lunch one day, *Time* magazine's Ozersky pointed at Bunk's Pork Belly Cubano and bellowed to no one in particular: "Way *WAY* better than anything in Miami." Habetz could cook any place, but Portland is now home: "It's the people, the livability, the lack of ego and pomp. That comes out in the music scene here; that's our style. No bullshit, non-polished. When all of that pretense is squashed, it puts pressure on quality, forces you to have something to say. No excuses. It's true of music, it's true of art, and it's true here."

Come and meet the zany cooks defying the gods of gastronomy. And, of course, enjoy the recipes, with their mashing of the savory and sweet, their testimonials to culinary archaeology, and their mining of the Great Chain of Being and Being Eaten. They are road maps to Portland's beating heart. Welcome to the Mighty Gastropolis. Pull up a seat. Valet parking? are you kidding?

CHAPTER 1

BEASTIE BOYS

A band of meat slayers carve out a world of pure, audacious delights. Welcome to Porklandia.

I LOVE ANIMALS
THEY'RE DELICIOUS

CUTS AVAILABLE TONIGHT:

- $15 CULOTTE
- 6/7 HANGER
- 1/2 TERES MAJOR
- 1/2 FLAT IRON
- 5 BRISKET
- 7/8/9 RIBEYE
- 10 SHORT RIBS
- $15 TOP SIRLOIN
- $15 BAVETTE

LE PIGEON

RALEIGH BAR
pecan·nougat·bourbon caramel

XOCOLATL

GABRIEL RUCKER

LE PIGEON +
LITTLE BIRD

Portland's premier gastro-basher creates his own offal Winfrey show.

New Year's Eve. A gritty stretch of East Burnside. A pile of lamb heads. A power drill.

These could have been the ingredients for a Stephen King novel. But on that winter day in 2006, just six months after Gabriel Rucker debuted at Le Pigeon, they proved to be the mix that enabled him to do what he loves: send delicious shivers up the spines of food-loving customers.

Earlier that day, Rucker huddled with his trusted side cook, Erik Van Kley, to face the problem of (literally) cracking into a free cache of lamb skulls. All agreed: Owner Paul Brady was "good with tools." Off Brady went to the basement kitchen, like a hit man in *Goodfellas*, to bore out the goods. Hours later, Rucker and Van Kley were frying up brains, tongues, and cheeks to mash with potatoes and mushrooms for Le Pigeon's new Lamb's Head Shepherd's Pie. It was more than a hit. Customers clamored for seconds.

If their clientele would eat up the innards of a lamb's noggin, Rucker had to ask: "Where do we go from here?" Answer: foie gras ice cream, barbecued pig's tail, soup with squab heads, and a menu that rocketed Rucker into the national spotlight at age twenty-six. Now, food-world heavyweights make pilgrimages to eat whatever results from the ideas that pop into his head.

The narrow space typifies how Portland's indie restaurant culture aspires to be fun but substantive. First, lose the French accent. Say *le pidge-en*. Just like the park bird. That's how Rucker pronounces Le Pigeon, the perch for his electric send-ups of French food. Here, thrift-store silverware shines alongside a serious Francophile wine list, and foie gras—a house obsession—rides out on a raft of brioche toast with a long-fingered, crispy-crunchy pigeon claw reaching up to greet you like a voodoo charm. By dinner's end, the block of corn bread resting under maple ice cream, warm porky bits, and bacon-infused maple syrup has you rethinking breakfast, dessert, and life all at once.

Rucker's having a ball, and he hopes you are, too. He struts about the joint with his pigeon tattoos and good-old-boy charm, sometimes delivering dishes by himself, thumbs crooked in his belt loops, hailing customers with a "you guys" familiarity, and belting out phrases like "I L-O-V-E lamb fat." He's the ringleader of this underground party, a density of serious feeders, off-duty chefs, and seniors who can live with

raucous music. But even regulars moan about the enforced communal eating in these tight quarters. It's a Portland way of life: to eat out is to know thy neighbor—and his wife.

The Genesis

Le Pigeon evolved from Colleen's Bistro, an early avatar of the obsessive handmade cooking, meat delirium, and do-it-yourself décor that put Portland on the national food map.

In early 2006, while many of her peers dreamed of vegan cheesecake, Colleen French was thinking about venison sausage. French was cooking breakfast for a cult in a closet-size hole-in-the-wall when a miracle occurred: Friend Paul Brady volunteered to finance her dream restaurant, with a real gas stove and hanging copper pots.

Colleen's Bistro, as she called it, became the outlet for French's real passion: mountain food. Wild boar burgers and goose pie joined her morning staples. French knew her mostly young crowd was uncomfortable with eating meat

and game. But she grew up with hunting kin. She could shoot a rifle, and her aim was true.

French decorated her funky bistro as a punk expression of the Parisian backstreet, with eerie glowing lanterns made of caul fat and sausage casings. From her open kitchen counter, she made her stand: "I want people to see the whole pork belly, to see us removing the skin. I want them to see the hair as we're cooking the bacon, the way it looks like a man who shaved his face but two days later. People say to me, 'What's that? Is that *hair*?' I say, 'Yes! Pigs have hair!!' It's important that people respect the food. I want people to know what they're eating."

Most Frequently Asked Question at Le Pigeon

"Are the pigeons from the park?"

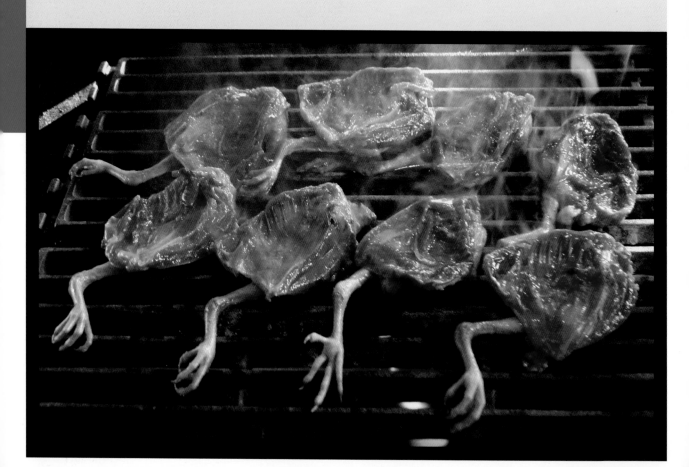

Colleen's cooking was nothing short of a foretaste of heaven, but as she fretted over every molecule of flavor, you could knock off a Tolstoy novel waiting for it. Exasperated customers fled. But compromise was out of the question. "Paul believes in me," said French.

April 2006
Hi, Karen:

Colleen said she told you that she was considering having an "in-house hunter" provide game meats from time to time. We just found out that this would be a federal offense. Needless to say, there will be no in-house hunter at Colleen's Bistro.

Sincerely,
Paul and Colleen

By June, Brady no longer believed, telling French that something had to change: her high-cost slow-food approach was bleeding money. She bolted, announcing that their friendship would live on but vowing, "I'm taking my from-scratch approach with me." (French was last seen in California cooking a renegade dinner "in a ruined Los Feliz mansion," according to an Internet report.)

Into this chaos, on a tip and a lark, entered twenty-five-year-old Gabriel Rucker, an unknown line cook rumored to be the next great talent among coworkers at the Gotham Building Tavern. Once again, Brady flashed the idealism that had inspired him to mortgage his house to finance Colleen's Bistro. Without even tasting Rucker's food, he hired him on the spot because he "liked his ideas."

In Portland, it's not who you know or where you've cooked. It's about feelin' it. Within a year, Rucker was the poster boy for Portland's emergence on the national scene.

Winging It at the Stove

Le Pigeon's maestro and mischief maker cooks without recipes, everything on the fly, everything going down in real time. Working in his own world of complex combinations, Rucker toys with France, roams America's highways, and combs the Asian streets, sometimes all in the same dish. It's hard to know what is coming your way on any dish, as brief menu annotations like "duck, crêpe, chard, peaches & foie" only hint at what Rucker has up his sleeve. The astute just ask the man to deliver and watch the surprises unfold. A night's catch might include sturgeon, date jam, and hot chile oil dots, or sweetbreads swaddled in Carolina barbecue sauce, crowned with smoked cherries, bread pudding on the side.

The heart of Rucker's cooking is, well, hearts . . . and tails and marrow bones and other spare body parts. The word "trotters!" is hand scrawled and taped to his front burners. Great knobs of charred, tender meat stand at the center of his transcendent Beef Cheek Bourguignon. Foie gras punctuates his most daring ideas, including the suave surprise of foie gras ice cream scooped into cream puffs honking with foie gras caramel and foie gras powdered sugar. During one stretch he fixated on crispy, crunchy, salt-singing fried duck necks, calling them "like the best part of Thanksgiving over and over."

How Wild Does It Get?

Pig's foot, bacon soup, barbecued pork tongue: "Our 'pho' with trotters. Pork tongue is pretty mild, but it's a bitch to peel, and trust me, I've peeled them all."

Blood-noodle ravioli: "The idea of pasta with pig's blood came right out of my head one night. Blood has that great iron-y flavor and a good color. It's a bit of a shazam, a whistle, but people f---ing loved it."

Beef-lip-stuffed squash blossoms, seared monkfish, tomato jam: "I like to cook with things no one uses, to make delicious things with ingredients people throw in the garbage. Lips have amazing beef flavor without being overpowering, and they love tomato products. I just served them to people paying $10,000 a plate . . . I just didn't tell them until the end."

But he loves nothing as much as he does squab (pigeon). When the restaurant needed a name, he looked down at his arm, and there it was, inked in cursive script, a two-word synopsis of his love of French food: *le pigeon*. He has other tattoos, too: a can of deviled ham, a sly-smiling shark, and a giant stick of butter. That pretty much sums it up.

The French Connection

Here's Rucker's resume in a nutshell: Born in Napa Valley; country-club cook at age nineteen; number of trips to France: zero. His most European experience was a two-year stint at Paley's Place, a beloved French-Northwest bistro above a hair salon on Portland's west side. He once bought Escoffier's *Le Guide Culinaire*, the Talmud of French cuisine, but his cat peed on it. Nevertheless, Rucker has an uncanny feel for French flavors, turning out a veal blanquette as satisfying as something made by the big boys in Paris.

Rucker's flavors penetrate deep, not just "earthy" but more like a journey to the center of the earth. Like a competitor on *Iron Chef*, he deploys unexpected ingredients in multiple formats in one dish, layering the essence in a style he calls "dirty French." In one creation, caraway shoots through rye-flavored "Parisienne" gnocchi, braised rabbit hindquarters, and fennel sauerkraut, and that's after you rake your fork through chilled matchsticks of pickled caraway carrots. The whole thing is kind of an epiphanic shock— Left Bank, Jewish deli, and *bánh mì* sandwich shop, are you kidding?—but it works. These nuanced ideas are born out of pure instinct, and they hold the key to Rucker's genius.

From Park Bird to Songbird

In 2011, on his fourth round in the nomination ring, Rucker finally knocked out tough national competition to win the coveted James Beard Rising Star Chef of the Year award, aimed at hotshots under thirty. Rising-star chefs are often understudies of superstars like Thomas Keller, not culinary school dropouts running a low-budget bistro on a sketchy boulevard. Days later, Portland's prince of fine-dining-gone-grunge found his lusty burger leaping off the pages of *People* magazine.

Cult status often means a date with the Food Network or a vanity project to feed the ego. But even before the Beard award, Rucker had passed on opportunities to appear on top-rated food shows. He's happy in front of the camera but happier in front of the stove cooking with his friends. He even created a home for them at Little Bird, his second venture, located in the heart of downtown.

Little Bird skips the DIY décor for tush-friendly banquettes and more familiar French food under longtime collaborator Van Kley. But touches of Northwest noir leave no doubt that this is Portlandia, not Provence: Stuffed birds hide in portal holes, mossy plants sprout out of mirrors, and what counts as a thrilling vista is the passing MAX train on the bus mall outside. The kitchen throws enough sideways glances to keep things interesting, including a pair of hulking veal marrow bones that look on loan from a natural history museum. You eat them as if excavating a tunnel, spooning out the roasted, jelly-soft essence, inhaling deep whiffs of balsamic-glazed onions, and then slurping it all up. It's primal enough to make you blush.

Rucker's Rules:

- Cheaper cuts of meat are the most fun.

- Take it low and slow. Braise meats overnight in a 175°F/80°C oven.

- Salt, fat, and acid are the holy trinity. Put them in everything.

- Salt every step of the way to build flavor and depth as you go. Even sautéed onions should be salted.

- Sugar is one-dimensional, a surface flavor. Use honey or maple sugar for depth.

- Add a big squeeze of lemon at the end for that bright taste.

- Use multiple vinegars to deepen sauces and vinaigrettes. Favorite trio: muscatel (sweetness), white balsamic (complexity), and apple cider vinegar (tang).

But everyone finds something to love. At Little Bird, power brokers can eat a wee bit dangerously; and daters and cleavage are arriving in force. Half of the diners are eating a well-behaved duck confit you'd be happy to introduce to your mother, and no one is hollering for more fried cow's tongue, the kitchen's slowest seller.

Meanwhile, across the river at Le Pigeon, Gabriel Rucker still ruffles feathers.

Epilogue

Rucker is now the proud father of Augustus Lee Lightningbolt Rucker, whose first solid food was foie gras.

ARUGULA AND PLUM SALAD WITH PECORINO DRESSING

For all its meat savvy, Le Pigeon turns out greatly imagined salads. This one comes with two components, two kinds of pepper in two dressings and a double dose of whole lemons and shaved cheese everywhere. But the creamy pecorino drizzled over plums alongside dressed greens shows how even a simple salad can transcend the ordinary. Leftover dressings shouldn't go to waste; save them for dipping vegetables or dressing other leaves.

Pecorino Dressing

1 tsp white peppercorns

2/3 cup/165 ml muscatel vinegar or sweet wine vinegar

2 egg yolks

1 tsp kosher salt

1 cup/240 ml vegetable oil

2/3 cup/165 ml olive oil

1/4 cup plus 1 tbsp/45 g freshly grated aged pecorino cheese

Lemon-Pepper Dressing

1 tsp black peppercorns

5 lemons, peeled, seeded, and coarsely chopped

1 cup/240 ml extra-virgin olive oil

1 tsp minced fresh thyme

2 small shallots, finely chopped

1 tsp kosher salt

Salad

4 medium plums

12 oz/340 g arugula, washed and dried

Extra-virgin olive oil for drizzling

Fleur de sel for garnish

3 oz/85 g aged pecorino cheese

1. TO MAKE THE PECORINO DRESSING: In a dry skillet, toast the white peppercorns over medium-high heat until fragrant, about 2 minutes. In a spice grinder, pulverize the peppercorns to a medium-coarse powder.

2. In a blender, combine the vinegar, egg yolks, salt, and white pepper. With the blender running, slowly drizzle in both the oils, 1 tbsp at a time, blending well after each addition. After 1/2 cup/120 ml oil has been added and the dressing has begun to emulsify (come together and thicken), add up to 1/4 cup/60 ml oil at a time and blend until fully incorporated. Transfer the dressing to a medium bowl and stir in the cheese. Set aside.

3. TO MAKE THE LEMON-PEPPER DRESSING: In a dry skillet, toast the black peppercorns over medium-high heat until fragrant, about 2 minutes. In a spice grinder, pulverize the peppercorns to a medium-coarse powder.

4. In a blender, purée the lemons, olive oil, and ground pepper and transfer the mixture to a medium bowl. Fold in the thyme, shallots, and salt. Set aside.

5. TO PREPARE THE SALAD: Cut each plum into quarters, then cut each quarter lengthwise into three wedges for a total of forty-eight wedges. In a medium bowl, toss the plums with 1/4 cup/60 ml of the pecorino dressing.

6. In a large bowl, toss the arugula with 3 tbsp of the lemon-pepper dressing. Mound a handful onto each of six plates, fluffing up the leaves for height. Nestle four plum wedges into the greens and arrange four more plum wedges on the perimeter between one and three o'clock on the plate. Spoon a little more of the pecorino dressing over the plums on the perimeter, letting it puddle beneath. Drizzle the greens with extra-virgin olive oil and finish with a sprinkling of fleur de sel. Using a vegetable peeler, shave pecorino in a light layer over each salad before serving.

SERVES 6

BBQ PIGEON AND DIRTY POTATO SALAD

When challenged to create a dish on the spot for this book, Rucker took all of five seconds. His thought process: "I just look around the kitchen, grab a tub of something, and go!" Without warning, alongside a plastic bin holding balsamic vinegar, Thai hot sauce, and mayonnaise, he decapitated six birds. (Guess who almost fainted, and it wasn't Rucker.) Soon, heads were bobbing in an Asian-French-American-Something barbecue sauce, innards were lacing a "dirty" potato salad, and the birds, claws and all, were aflame on a grill, looking like a vision from Burning Man. The final plate is a painterly vision of scallion shreds, flying feet, and hot red peppers, with swooping flavors: tart, sharp, fruity, crazy. If you want to try this at home, your butcher can always do the, er, dirty work to prep the birds. Just don't leave the body parts behind.

Potato Salad

1½ lb/680 g Yukon gold potatoes, scrubbed

One 4-lb/1.8-kg box rock salt

1 tbsp dried hot red pepper flakes

5 sprigs fresh tarragon

5 sprigs fresh thyme

1 orange

4 whole scallions (white and green portions), thinly sliced

2 celery stalks, thinly sliced

2 sweet red jalapeños, seeded, thinly sliced; or ⅓ cup/70 g thinly sliced red bell pepper

½ cup/120 ml mayonnaise

2 tsp Chinese mustard

1 tsp Sriracha sauce

Kosher salt

Juice of 1 lemon

¼ cup/60 ml Bird BBQ Sauce (page 30)

1 tbsp olive oil (optional)

Innards of 6 squabs (optional)

1 tbsp balsamic vinegar (optional)

Grilled Squab

2 tsp kosher salt

2 tsp olive oil

6 squabs, cleaned (innards reserved) and butterflied, with claws attached

½ cup/120 ml Bird BBQ Sauce (page 30)

3 scallions (green portion only), thinly sliced, for garnish

1. TO MAKE THE POTATO SALAD: Preheat the oven to 400°F/200°C/gas 6. Place the potatoes in a 13-by-9-in/33-by-23-cm roasting pan. Cover with the rock salt, dried hot red pepper flakes, tarragon, and thyme. Cut 1-in-/2.5-cm-wide strips of rind from half of the orange and toss in, reserving the orange for garnishing the plate. Cover tightly with foil and roast until the potatoes are fork tender, 45 to 60 minutes.

2. Remove the pan from the oven and let cool. Remove the potatoes, brushing off the salt. (Remove and discard the orange peel and herbs; save the rock salt for another use.) Place the potatoes on a cutting board and smash gently with your palm to break them up. Put into a large bowl and add the scallions, celery, and two-thirds of the jalapeño (reserving the remaining one-third for garnishing the final dish). Stir in the mayonnaise, mustard, Sriracha, 1 tsp salt, lemon juice, and bbq sauce.

3. Peel and separate six sections of the reserved orange. Cut each section lengthwise into three thin slices and set aside. Using your hand, squeeze the juice from the remaining orange over the bowl of potato mixture and discard the rind.

4. If using the innards, heat a small sauté pan over medium-high heat and add the olive oil. Add the innards (stand back; it will spatter) and sauté for 1 minute, shaking the pan continuously. Remove the innards and drain the oil from the pan. Add the balsamic vinegar to the pan, return to medium heat, and cook until reduced by half, about 1 minute. Coarsely chop the innards and stir into the vinegar. Add the innards to the potato salad and toss gently with your hands to incorporate. Season with salt and serve at room temperature, or cover and refrigerate overnight.

5. TO PREPARE THE SQUABS: Heat a charcoal grill to medium-hot. Rub the salt and olive oil over the birds, and place them skin-side down on the grill. Cook for 1 minute, then turn the birds over and brush them generously with the bbq sauce. Cook for about 30 seconds, being careful not to scorch the squabs if flames flare up, then turn again and brush with more sauce. In the case of flare-ups, remove the squabs from the grill until the flames die down, or move them to another part of the grill where the flames are lower. Continue turning every minute or so, brushing with sauce each time, until medium-rare, 4 to 5 minutes. Don't overcook or the birds will develop a ferric flavor.

6. Lightly brush a wide streak of the remaining bbq sauce in the center of each of six plates. Mound some potato salad in the middle. Then lean a squab over the top, slightly off center, with the claws reaching for the sky. Sprinkle a generous amount of sliced scallion greens and a few slices of the reserved jalapeño or red pepper over the top. Finish by nestling a few of the reserved sliced orange segments on the side before serving.

SERVES 6

GRILLED STEAK WITH BACON-ROASTED MUSHROOMS AND BLACK TRUMPET BUTTER

Dishes may be off-the-cuff at Le Pigeon, but that doesn't mean they're simplistic. Even steak is truly special, constructed in cunning Le Pigeon mode: propped like a lean-to over garlic-roasted potatoes, encircled by sweet and smoky mushrooms, and capped with wild mushroom butter.

Bacon-Roasted Mushrooms

1 medium red onion, thinly sliced

6 garlic cloves, sliced

1¼ lb/570 g cremini mushrooms, quartered

¼ lb/115 g smoked slab bacon, cut into chunks

10 fresh sage leaves, roughly chopped

⅓ cup/75 ml sherry vinegar

1¼ tsp kosher salt

½ cup/120 ml pure maple syrup

2 cups/480 ml veal or beef stock

2 tbsp unsalted butter, at room temperature

Roasted Potatoes

2 lb/910 g fingerling potatoes, halved lengthwise

1 tsp kosher salt

8 garlic cloves, halved lengthwise

2 tbsp olive oil

Grilled Steak

2½-lb/1.2-kg slab flatiron steak

Kosher salt and freshly ground black pepper

Six ½-in-/12-mm-thick slices Gabriel's Black Trumpet Butter, at room temperature (recipe follows)

2 tsp minced fresh parsley

Aged balsamic vinegar for drizzling

Fleur de sel for finishing

1. TO MAKE THE MUSHROOMS: Preheat the oven to 400°F/200°C/gas 6.

2. In a deep, flameproof roasting pan, combine the onion, garlic, mushrooms, bacon, sage, vinegar, salt, maple syrup, and stock. Bring to a boil over high heat, stirring frequently. Transfer to the oven and roast until the mushrooms are tender and the bacon is cooked, about 1 hour. Stir in the butter and set aside.

3. TO ROAST THE POTATOES: After the mushrooms have roasted for about 20 minutes, heat a baking sheet in the same oven for 10 minutes.

4. In a large bowl, toss the potatoes with the salt, garlic, and olive oil. Transfer the mixture to the hot baking sheet and roast until golden brown, 20 to 30 minutes.

5. TO PREPARE THE STEAK: Remove the steak from the refrigerator 30 minutes before cooking. Heat a charcoal grill to medium-hot or heat a large cast-iron skillet over high heat. (If skillet is not large enough to hold the steak, cut the meat in half and cook in batches, keeping the first steak warm while the second steak is cooking.)

6. Generously season both sides of the meat with salt and pepper. Cook the steak until medium-rare, 3 to 5 minutes per side, depending on the thickness of the steak. Transfer to a cutting board, loosely tent with aluminum foil, and let rest for 5 minutes.

7. Preheat the broiler. Using a long, sharp knife, cut the steak against the grain into ½-in-/12-mm-thick slices.

8. Mound a few potatoes in the center of six ovenproof plates. Spoon some of the bacon-roasted mushrooms over the potatoes, drizzling a little of the mushroom liquid around the plate. Place three or four slices of steak, slightly overlapping, and top with a slice of black trumpet butter. Broil just until the butter is slightly melted, about 20 seconds. Sprinkle with the parsley. Drizzle the balsamic vinegar and sprinkle fleur de sel around the edges of each plate before serving.

SERVES 6

GABRIEL'S BLACK TRUMPET BUTTER

Oregon black trumpet mushrooms, prized for their smoky-fruity aroma, are the stars of Le Pigeon's balsamic-streaked compound butter. Make a day ahead if possible; the butter slices up perfectly when frozen. Cut off thin rounds as needed to cap off anything in need of a woodsy jump, from steak to pasta to chicken.

3 tbsp olive oil
1 medium onion, thinly sliced
12 oz/340 g black trumpet or other wild mushrooms, torn into small pieces
1 cup/225 g salted butter, at room temperature
1 tsp aged balsamic vinegar

1. In a large sauté pan, warm 1 tbsp of the olive oil over medium heat. Add the onion, reduce the heat to medium-low, and cook, stirring frequently, until golden brown and caramelized, about 30 minutes. Transfer to a bowl and set aside.

2. Heat the remaining olive oil in the same skillet over medium heat. Add the mushrooms and sauté, stirring frequently, until tender, about 10 minutes. Remove and cool completely.

3. In a food processor, purée the butter, onions, and mushrooms until smooth. Transfer to a sheet of parchment or wax paper and, using a spatula, form the butter into a 6-by-3-in/15-by-7.5-cm rectangle that ends 1 in/2.5 cm away from the lower edge of the paper. Drizzle the balsamic vinegar over the top of the butter. Lift the lower edge of the paper up and over the butter, enclosing the vinegar into the butter. Tuck the edge of the paper under the butter and continue rolling up the paper around the butter tightly to form a log, smoothing it out with your hands. Twist the ends of the paper to seal. Freeze for up to one month.

MAKES ABOUT 1 LB/455 G

FOIE GRAS BUTTER

Why stop at plain butter when you can double the pleasure with foie gras? At Le Pigeon, it perfumes ice cream *and* steaks.

1 cup/225 g unsalted butter, cut into
1-in/2.5-cm cubes, at room temperature

4 oz/115 g uncooked foie gras, cut into
1-in/2.5-cm cubes, at room temperature

1. Preheat the oven to 325°F/165°C/gas 3.

2. Place the butter and foie gras in a small baking dish and cover with foil. Warm in the oven until slightly softened, about 5 minutes. Transfer to a food processor and blend until smooth, about 40 seconds. Refrigerate in a covered container up to 5 days or freeze up to 1 month.

MAKES 12 OZ/340 G

BIRD BBQ SAUCE

Rucker swears he can't tell the difference between Texas- and Carolina-style barbecue. He just knows he loves barbecue sauce, and he lives to make up his own. Condiments and fruit often figure into formulas never repeated twice. Here, he brings Chinese mustard and prune juice into a vision of sweet, deep, and dark. Swab this concoction on ribs or chicken before grilling. Or try the BBQ Pigeon (see page 26) and get into full Rucker mode, adding the squab heads to the sauce as it reduces.

1 tbsp olive oil

½ medium red onion, finely diced

5 garlic cloves, thinly sliced

Kosher salt

Heaping 1 tbsp brown sugar

½ cup/120 ml ketchup

2 tbsp Chinese hot mustard

Zest and juice of ½ orange

½ cup/120 ml prune juice

½ cup/120 ml balsamic vinegar

3 tbsp hoisin sauce

6 squab heads (optional)

2 tsp freshly squeezed lemon juice

In a medium saucepan over medium heat, warm the olive oil. Add the onion and garlic and sauté, stirring, until the onion is translucent, about 5 minutes. Add 1 tsp salt, brown sugar, ketchup, hot mustard, orange zest and juice, prune juice, vinegar, and hoisin sauce. (If using the squab heads, add here.) Bring to a boil and reduce by half, stirring often, for 10 minutes. Add the lemon juice and season with salt. (Remove the bird heads and discard.) Refrigerate in a covered container up to 1 week.

MAKES ¾ CUP/180 ML

LE PIGEON'S FOIE GRAS PROFITEROLES

It takes a thick hide to put foie gras in ice cream *and* caramel sauce that's lavished over tiny profiterole shells. Like most things at Le Pigeon, it makes you laugh, debate, and wallow in the sheer, unexpected joy of it all. For home use, we've substituted bakery or store-bought profiteroles for Le Pigeon's foie gras–buttered version and bypassed the labor-intensive finale of foie gras powdered sugar. Rest assured, even when the recipe is simplified, decadent flavor is not in shortage. The caramel sauce alone is fantastic on ice cream, finished with fleur de sel and chocolate shavings. Look for more affordable raw foie gras "chunks" online at Nicky USA, Hudson Valley Foie Gras, or D'artagnan.

Foie Gras Caramel Sauce

1 cup/200 g sugar

¼ cup/60 ml water

1 cup/240 ml heavy cream

4 oz/115 g Foie Gras Butter (facing page), at room temperature

Foie Gras Ice Cream

8 oz/225 g uncooked foie gras, cut into 1-in/2.5-cm cubes

¼ cup/60 ml dry white port

½ cup/100 g sugar

2 egg yolks

½ cup/115 g unsalted butter, cut into small pieces, at room temperature

½ cup/120 g heavy cream, at room temperature

Profiteroles

18 store-bought or homemade profiterole shells

¼ cup/15 g bittersweet chocolate shavings for garnish

Fleur de sel for sprinkling

1. TO MAKE THE CARAMEL SAUCE: Combine the sugar and water in a medium saucepan. Without stirring, cook over medium-high heat, swirling the pan to cook evenly, until the color is deep amber, 8 to 10 minutes. Slowly add the cream and stir quickly with a heat-proof spatula (be careful—the mixture will bubble vigorously and splatter), scraping the caramel from the bottom of the pan and cooking a few more minutes to melt the hardened bits.

2. Remove from the heat and stir in the butter. Transfer to a bowl and let it cool completely. Cover and store in the refrigerator for up to 1 week. Before serving, warm the caramel slightly in a small saucepan over low heat.

3. TO MAKE THE FOIE GRAS ICE CREAM: Preheat the oven to 275°F/135°C/gas 1.

4. Put the foie gras in a small baking dish, cover with foil, and render in the oven until slightly melted, about 10 minutes. Meanwhile, place a medium stainless-steel bowl over (*not* in) a pot of simmering water. Pour the port into the bowl and whisk in the sugar and egg yolks. Continue heating and whisking until the mixture reaches a ribbon stage, 6 to 8 minutes. (When you lift the whisk, the mixture should make a long, thick stream or "ribbon.")

5. Transfer the egg mixture to a food processor. With the processor running, slowly add the rendered foie gras. Add the butter, one piece at a time, until completely incorporated. Using a fine-mesh sieve, strain over a medium bowl. Whisk in the cream.

6. Pour the warm cream mixture into an ice-cream maker and freeze according to the manufacturer's directions. As soon as it begins to thicken, stop the machine. Be careful not to overchurn. It should have the consistency of thick taffy. Transfer to a covered container and freeze overnight.

7. TO ASSEMBLE THE PROFITEROLES: In a small saucepan, gently warm the caramel sauce over low heat. Slice the profiteroles in half crosswise and place three bottom halves on each of six plates. Place a small scoop of ice cream inside the bottom half and cap with the top half. Spoon some warm caramel over each, and finish with a little shaved chocolate and fleur de sel. Serve immediately.

SERVES 6

TOMMY HABETZ

BUNK SANDWICHES + BUNK BAR

From Batali's army,
a sandwich hero rises.

Bunk Sandwiches looks like the man cave in someone's garage: a boom box, a cramped blackboard menu, and a few tables staring at stacked cardboard boxes. There's no stove in sight, just hot plates, a sandwich press, and some industrial gear from a pawnshop. The culinary vision is summed up by a photo on its website: a flap of bacon protruding from a fried-egg sandwich like Mick Jagger's tongue. Pork belly Reubens and po'boys dripping duck gravy arrive on paper-lined snack trays, and the whoopie pies are made by someone called Sugar Pimp. A perpetual line snakes through the smoky haze. Suits and tattoos, construction hunks, even a few spice-loving elders, canes in hand, are in it together, looking for instant bliss on bread, and no one seems to mind the takeaway perfume: eau de pork.

Tommy Habetz isn't climbing culinary ladders or waiting for his spread in the *New York Times*. He's the new face of a culinary world remaking itself amid economic recalibration and celebrity-chef overdose. Over a decade ago, Habetz worked with the brightest stars in the biz. He bailed from New York's restaurant world (and jobs with rising stars Mario Batali and Bobby Flay). Now he lives his own dream, transforming the humble sandwich into a kind of ecstatic, don't-eat-this-while-operating-machinery, objet d'art served with camaraderie and a punk aesthetic.

Fame has found him anyway. Bunk's meaty, working-class heroes are food-porn faves in national magazines. The kitchen's audacious Pork Belly Cubano had a star turn on *The Best Thing I Ever Ate*, where dimpled host Chris Cosentino boisterously called it "way, way better" than the original roast pork and ham combo.

Meanwhile, Habetz and his hoagies have turned up in the weighty tome *Coco: 10 World-Leading Masters Choose 100 Contemporary Chefs*. In a gastro-compendium as heavy as a small child, ten members of the global fooderati ordained chefs pushing their craft to new heights. Habetz's three-page spread is a startling site, his unstudied arrangement of oxtail confit, hot-pepper relish, and crusty bread hanging out among the lavishly photographed fashion plates from the new gastronomic elite. But there it is, Bunk, the zeitgeist of Portland; Habetz and his world of heavenly tuna melts have raised the bar for low-brow cuisine no one can resist.

How did Portland's sandwich king land in such lofty company? Batali selected him. After all, the two go way

back. Habetz stood alongside the orange-Croced Visigoth in his prefame days at Po and Lupa. (Today, the only people standing alongside Molto Mario have names like Gwyneth.) Writes Batali of his former protégé, the man he calls Puff Daddy Habetz: "Sure, making a sandwich seems simple enough to do, especially for a noted chef, but taking the sandwich to an art form and making a city demand it day after day takes true genius. When we opened Lupa together, I could count on his simple flair with pasta to be a technical score that I did not have to worry about. Having worked through the fun at high-end restaurants, Puff granted the wishes of those who love simple gustatory pleasures like a sandwich. Habetz's knack for understanding and creating food for everyone is a great achievement."

The secret to Bunk? It doesn't take itself seriously while delivering serious flavors. Habetz can conjure Roman cuisine, East Coast deli juju, and Asian street food seemingly at will. His culinary partner, Nick Wood, has a gut instinct for Southern soul. Together, they create like rock stars, minus the egos. Bread is simply their drum kit. "What we offer is high-level food with a low level of BS," says Habetz. "It's refreshing coming from New York."

From Moosewood to Mario

Behind the maverick short-order life, the rumpled tuft of sandy hair, and the flannel shirts is a man with abiding interests in film, music, and literature. But Habetz's earliest influence was, of all things, *The Moosewood Cookbook*, an icon of hippie vegetarian cooking. He was a student at Connecticut's Natural Gourmet cooking school in 1992 when a teacher told him to "check out a guy named Mario doing interesting stuff in the West Village." He headed to New York, but detoured to the Mesa Grill, the springboard for Bobby Flay's march to superstardom.

Surviving Mesa's relentless crowds was a daily fire fight, as cooks ended shifts with sweat-drenched shirts and thousand-yard stares. Here, Habetz earned a tasting rigor that caught Batali's attention, and then a job offer at Po. Though he rarely encountered Flay, he remembers one of his last shifts at Mesa. Recalls Habetz: "He looked up and said, 'What the f——— are you always smiling about?' I guess I was just happy. His friend Mario had just hired me."

Why Guy Fieri Matters

Habetz is laid back, comic, and droll, a little cynical and deeply moral, like Detective Bunk Moreland, a character on the HBO drama series *The Wire*. Bunk Moreland is the muse for Bunk Sandwiches and Bunk Bar, a nighttime spin-off with antimixology drinking and live underground music. It's the kind of a place where you might stumble on *Portlandia*'s Carrie Brownstein performing in rocker-girl mode, with the kitchen doubling as "the green room."

Diners, Drive-Ins and Dives, a Food Network show, loves places like Bunk Sandwiches. When the shop opened in 2009, bleached-blond host Guy Fieri dropped by "to find the funk in Bunk," calling Habetz and Wood "two dudes scratch-cooking not-so-ordinary sandwiches."

"We make what we like," says Wood, talking about their love of tripe, tongue, or salt cod puréed with potatoes and heaped on crispy bread with a "salad" of Italian parsley, chorizo, and black olives. Influential foodists, like outspoken chef/TV host Anthony Bourdain, love to rip Fieri, who looks like a heavy-metal spoof straight out of *Spinal Tap*. But Habetz sees a goofball focused on what counts: the food, techniques, and traditions found in small places.

"People love that show," says Habetz. "That's the thing. Food media people have this idea about hierarchy in food. There's been this elitism. Gourmet is dead. People are realizing the art in low-brow food. What I do now is just as valid as what I did before. There's no hierarchy if you're true to yourself. Some people consider Thomas Keller the end-all and be-all. But Keller is no more valid than the person making the best fried chicken in the South."

The Bunk Method

When is a classic something more than tradition and the personal poetry of taste memory? When it's pushed to become something greater, still recognizable but with a fresh stamp, something unexpected to record in the mouth's hall of fame. That's a Bunk sandwich. It's Korean fried chicken reborn with kim chee mayo or a *bánh mì* remade with pork meatballs and duck liver pâté. The outline begins here:

- Start with something authentic. Even a dive-shop classic can be upgraded with slow-cooked meats, intensely flavored marinades, or playful condiments.

- Treat condiments as a punctuation mark. Use plastic squirt bottles to add Jackson Pollock–esque squiggles to the bread—a method Habetz learned from Batali.
- Go bold and deep. Add something unexpected to the marinades or condiments—nutmeg, molasses, or, yes, even bacon fat, which hides inside Bunk's Russian Dressing like a roadside IED.
- Embrace the pork belly. Its rich fat bastes the meat, transforming it into a whole new animal.
- Crisp the bread. Bunk sandwiches are brushed with butter and panini grilled, which seals the deal with addictive crunchy edges.

Keeping It Real

Bunk is already fielding offers from deep pockets to franchise Bunk Bar in Los Angeles. But jumping into the big leagues is not a goal. More money would mean fancier equipment, sure, but Habetz and Wood are happy with what they have. Bunk made it happen with minimal means. The way Habetz sees it, "When you strip everything away, moments of beauty and transcendence are easier to see."

The next step, they say, must feel real, authentic—Portland to the core. But fate is always tempting. Habetz says he must conclude our conversation: *GQ* magazine is waiting on the phone.

BUNK'S
PORK BELLY CUBANO

At first glance, this looks like a straight-up reprise of the Cuban working man's ham and cheese sandwich. But one substitution alone earned it a shout-out on the Food Network's *The Best Thing I Ever Ate*: switching molasses-rubbed, flavor-rich pork belly for the conventional roast pork. Bunk's plan includes an overnight marinade, a three-hour oven roasting, and a final ride in a panini press for that full-on crispy finish. Like everything at Bunk, the "best thing you've ever eaten" gets a humble delivery treatment: on cafeteria trays heaped with salted Kettle Chips, a locally made favorite.

Pork Belly

1 cup/200 g kosher salt

1 cup/200 g sugar

1 tsp ground fennel seeds

1 tsp ground chile flakes

1 tsp ground nutmeg

1 large garlic clove, peeled and halved

One 3-lb/1.4-kg slab pork belly, skin removed

¼ cup/60 ml molasses

Sandwiches

Six 6-in/15-cm French buns, halved lengthwise

¼ cup plus 2 tbsp/80 ml high-quality mayonnaise

¼ cup/50 ml American yellow mustard

2 tsp hot sauce

Kosher salt

10 oz/280 g Swiss cheese, thinly sliced

10 oz/280 g smoked ham, thinly sliced

3 garlic-dill pickles, thinly sliced lengthwise

¼ cup/55 g melted butter

1. TO MAKE THE PORK BELLY: In a medium bowl, combine the salt, sugar, fennel seeds, chile flakes, and nutmeg. Rub the raw garlic halves over the pork and discard. Sprinkle the spice mixture over the pork to coat well. Transfer to a large sealable bag (or a covered roasting dish) to marinate in the refrigerator overnight or up to 24 hours.

2. An hour before roasting, remove the pork belly from the refrigerator to bring up to room temperature.

3. Preheat the oven to 275°F/135°C/gas 1.

4. Place the belly in a shallow roasting pan, meat-side down, and brush the top with the molasses. Place a piece of parchment paper over the meat and cover the pan tightly with foil. Roast until fork-tender, about 3 hours.

5. TO ASSEMBLE THE SANDWICHES: Heat a panini grill or large cast-iron skillet until hot. Using a sharp knife, cut the pork crosswise into six ¼-in-/6-mm-thick slices, then cut each slice in half, reserving the remaining pork belly for another use.

6. Open the buns and spread or squirt about 1½ tsp mayonnaise and 1 tsp mustard over each half. Drizzle with a few dashes of hot sauce and sprinkle with salt. On each bottom half, layer slices of cheese, ham, pork belly, and pickles. Cover with the tops and brush the outside of each bun with melted butter.

7. In batches, place the filled buns in the panini grill, pressing down to flatten them slightly. If using a cast-iron skillet, put another heavy skillet or weight on top to flatten them and turn them over after 2 or 3 minutes. Grill until golden brown. Serve immediately.

MAKES 6 SANDWICHES

TAGLIATELLE WITH UNCLE MARGARET'S CHICKEN LIVER RAGU

Before debuting at Portland's Ripe Supper Club, Tommy Habetz's legendary pasta dish helped put another restaurant on the map: New York's celebrated Lupa. Habetz says he drew from fond memories of Rome and chicken liver crostini whipped up alongside his mentor Mario Batali at Po in the West Village. Think chicken liver mousse tossed with brandy and cream smashed into a rustic sauce. What could be bad?

½ lb/225 g chicken livers, trimmed

Kosher salt

3 large garlic cloves, gently smashed

1 tbsp brandy

4 fresh thyme sprigs, plus 1 tsp fresh thyme leaves

2 tbsp olive oil

1 small red onion, thinly sliced

2 oz/55 g pancetta, roughly chopped

1 whole anchovy, rinsed

2 tsp tomato paste

3 fresh sage leaves, thinly sliced

2 tsp sherry vinegar

1 tbsp sweet vermouth

⅓ cup/80 ml heavy cream

2 lb/910 g fresh tagliatelle pasta

1. In a small bowl, combine the chicken livers with ½ tsp salt, 2 smashed garlic cloves, the brandy, and thyme sprigs. Marinate for 1 hour at room temperature, then remove and discard the garlic and thyme sprigs.

2. Bring a large pot of heavily salted water to a boil.

3. Meanwhile, dry the livers on paper towels. Heat a medium sauté pan over medium-high heat, and warm 1 tbsp of the olive oil. Add the livers (stand back; they'll splatter) and sauté, shaking the pan to toss the livers, until lightly brown, about 2 minutes on each side. Transfer to a plate.

4. Add the remaining 1 tbsp olive oil to the pan over medium heat. Add the onion and sauté until translucent, 10 to 12 minutes. Add ½ tsp salt and stir in the pancetta. Sauté, stirring often, until just cooked through, about 5 minutes. Add the anchovy and tomato paste, mashing with the back of a spoon and stirring to combine. Stir in the remaining garlic clove, thyme leaves, and sage and cook for 3 minutes, stirring often. Pour in the vinegar and vermouth, and cook 2 minutes, scraping the bottom of the pan with a wooden spoon. Stir in the livers and ½ tsp salt. Add the cream and bring to a simmer, stirring often. If you have an immersion blender, this would be a good time to use it; if not, transfer the mixture to a food processor or blender and purée until smooth. Transfer the ragu back to the pan and gently rewarm before serving.

5. Cook the pasta in the pot of boiling water until al dente (fresh pasta takes about 1 minute). Drain well, then divide the pasta equally among eight warm serving bowls. Spoon about ½ cup/120 ml of the ragu over each. Serve immediately. Store leftover sauce in a covered container in the refrigerator for up to 5 days.

SERVES 8

TOMMY'S MILK-BRAISED PORK SHOULDER

The Italian classic with improvements: deep-flavored shoulder in place of the typical loin, a back rub of fresh herbs and fennel, a cache of deep caramelized notes, and a final hit of freshly grated nutmeg.

1½ tsp fennel seeds

½ tsp dried chile flakes

7 large garlic cloves, coarsely chopped

1½ tsp chopped fresh rosemary

1 tbsp chopped fresh thyme

2 tsp fresh sage

Freshly grated nutmeg

Freshly ground black pepper

Kosher salt

5 tbsp/75 ml extra-virgin olive oil

One 3-lb/1.4-kg pork shoulder, trimmed

2 medium onions, thinly sliced

3 cups/720 ml whole milk

1. In a spice grinder, pulverize the fennel seeds and chile flakes until medium-fine. In a food processor, combine the garlic, rosemary, thyme, sage, nutmeg, a few grindings of black pepper, and 1 tbsp salt. Add the fennel-chile powder and 3 tbsp of the olive oil, and then pulse to combine.

2. Place the pork shoulder in a large, deep bowl. Rub the spice paste into the meat, lifting the flap to coat the entire shoulder. Cover the bowl with plastic wrap and refrigerate overnight, or up to 24 hours.

3. Remove the pork from the refrigerator an hour before roasting to bring it up to room temperature.

4. Preheat the oven to 450°F/230°C/gas 8.

5. In a roasting pan or Dutch oven large enough to hold the meat snugly, warm the remaining 2 tbsp olive oil over medium heat. Add the onions and ½ tbsp salt. Sauté over medium-low heat, stirring frequently, until the onions begin to color and slightly caramelize, about 25 minutes.

6. Place the meat on top of the onions and pour the milk over the top. Roast in the oven until a deep golden crust forms on the pork, about 45 minutes. Reduce the oven temperature to 350°F/180°C/gas 4. Turn the pork over and continue braising until fork-tender, 45 to 60 minutes.

7. Transfer the meat to a platter and cover with foil. Let rest for 15 minutes. Meanwhile, purée the milk and onions using an immersion blender or transfer the milk and onions to a food processor or blender and purée until smooth. Taste for salt and rewarm the sauce gently, if necessary. Cut the meat crosswise into ½-in-/12-mm-thick slices, transfer to a platter, and pour the sauce over the top to serve.

SERVES 8

BUNK'S MILK-BRAISED PORK AND WILTED MUSTARD GREENS SANDWICH

Essentially, this is an entrée and a side dish between two pieces of bread. It's classic Bunk, or, as Tommy Habetz calls it, "the ultimate chef's sandwich: pork and greens."

1 tbsp olive oil

2 garlic cloves, thinly sliced crosswise

1 tsp dried chile flakes

2 bunches mustard greens, center ribs removed

½ tsp kosher salt

Tommy's Milk-Braised Pork Shoulder (facing page), cooled and unsliced, sauce reserved

6 ciabatta rolls, halved crosswise

¼ cup/55 g butter, melted and slightly cooled

1. In a large sauté pan, heat the olive oil, garlic, and chile flakes over medium heat for 2 to 3 minutes. Add the greens and salt and cook, stirring frequently, until wilted, 3 to 4 minutes.

2. Meanwhile, slice the pork crosswise into about 24 thin slices. Spoon the sauce from the pork into another large sauté pan over medium-low heat. Add the meat to the sauce and gently warm for a few minutes.

3. Heat a panini grill or large cast-iron skillet until hot.

4. Open the rolls. Spoon 1 tbsp sauce over each half. Place three or four slices of meat on the bottom halves, and then cover with a small handful of the wilted greens. Cover with the tops and brush the outside of each roll with melted butter.

5. Place as many sandwiches in the panini grill as will fit, pressing down to flatten slightly. If using a cast-iron skillet, place a heavy skillet or weight on top to flatten, turning the sandwiches over after 2 to 3 minutes. Grill until golden brown. Serve immediately.

MAKES 6 SANDWICHES

THE BUTCHER BOYS

TORO BRAVO +
TASTY N SONS +
LAURELHURST
MARKET +
SIMPATICA

A collective of meat mavens carve out four bold dining destinations.

It began with the sudden appearance of an outsized leg of prosciutto swinging from a ceiling pipe like a shout-out from a Francis Bacon painting. Something interesting was simmering below a defunct rock club in Southeast Portland: Simpatica, a weekend supper club with rootsy American cooking and all-out animal bliss.

In 2005, as other cooks were tweaking the restaurant genre, John Gorham, Ben Dyer, and Jason Owens built a new model from scratch, open three days a week, and every meal a feast to remember. In short order, Simpatica opened the barnyard door for Portland's meat craze and comfort-food reformation. Home-cured bacons and crafty sausages paraded out of the kitchen in dishes that looked like mirages of the starving. No two menus were alike, then or now, but each one dug excitedly into the meat lockers of the rock 'n' roll butcher boys behind the scenes.

Sunday brunch emphasized this exuberance, with biscuits bathed in country gravy, waffles and fried chicken glistening with raisin syrup, and pampered meats from the trio's Viande butcher shop across the river. To land a coveted table, diners camped out in the hallway like rock concert hopefuls, eating rations from their pockets and sipping coffee from an emergency station at the door. Some were lured here by Dyer's folksy Internet newsletter, with its greeting of "Howdy" and virtual fist pumps to seasonal eating. Others found charm in the kitchen's open-door policy, wandering by chopping blocks and peering into skillets, a philosophy best expressed by Owens: "The kitchen is the engine. We don't see ourselves as separate from our customers."

While Owens held the reins for the brunch extravaganza, dinners belonged to Gorham and Dyer. For one night's feast, they rolled in a local pig, packed its belly with homegrown rosemary, marinated it for four days, and then spit-roasted the whole beast in a nearby alley with brushings of sauce full of ears and snouts just to punctuate the sheer porkiness of it all. On the side came corn bread, braised greens, and white-bean stew with double-smoked ham hocks. This was *after* the hush puppies, fried oysters, and bacon-wrapped shrimp and before the root-beer floats with homemade ice cream.

Gorham started cooking at age five, and his menus mash-up wherever life takes him. A Southern boy, he dive-bombs the deep fryer and frets over braises. He adopted

Italian cooking in San Francisco and African flavors on a Ghanaian journey. But his true love is Spanish food. In Gorham's world, tapas or "small plates" could be mistaken for hubcaps, with flavors to make your tongue laugh. For one night's "tapas dinner," he laid out thirteen dishes and a vigorous, knock-you-down paella—and just $25 for the whole shebang. *USA Today* declared the spread "The Best Meal in the World for 2006," ranking Simpatica one step ahead of the French Laundry.

For Gorham, the accolade was like God whispering "grab your inner bull by the horns." In 2007, he split from his partners at Simpatica to open Toro Bravo, a pig-snorting ode to Spain enabled by Oregon farmers and Gorham's charcuterie galore. Three years later, he hit another bull's-eye: In this breakfast-loving city, he boisterously redefined the genre at Tasty n Sons in gentrifying North Portland: fun and loud, with shared plates trumpeting spicy stews, North African sausages, and the house cry, "Put an egg on it."

In the late '90s, long before every Portland restaurant brandished a house charcuterie plate, John Gorham was busy transforming local pigs and lambs into fine sausages at Eugene's Café Zenon, an early advocate of whole-animal cooking. The kitchen overflowed with band saws and grinders, and Gorham was mesmerized by the primal, old-world ways. He saw the respect and it was a beautiful thing: bigger than life, a taste of civilization, a calling. He inked his newfound love on his left arm: a pinup girl whose body is dissected into "parts" (round, rump, and ribs among them) like a butcher's diagram.

Gorham seemingly mind-reads what we want to eat: comfort, craft, and value served with shotgun blasts of sweet, salty, spicy flavors. No one better translates Portland's raging gustatory desires. Toro Bravo, his natty little storefront in the middle of Nowheresville is always packed, popping with oxtail croquettes and smoked coppa steaks, and louder than a bullring. Hour-long waits are also the norm at Tasty n Sons, where meat rules and the Bloody Mary sports a swizzle stick of Tasty Beef Jerky.

Despite the crowds, a Gorham restaurant never has a whiff of the factory, the sense of cranking it out or phoning it in. Technique and complex seasonings are hidden tools in simple dishes that drill down to the yummy zone. Even the butter is fresh-churned to glaze over the house green beans,

a fact never mentioned on the menu. Money is the last motivation. Says Gorham: "I just want to feed souls. Everything real. I don't cheat at all."

John Gorham's No-Bull Kitchen Rules

- **Pamper your meats.** Salt and air-dry meat overnight on a rack or butcher paper. "The salt penetrates the meat, water is released, and the meat concentrates into something deeper and richer."

- **Experiment.** Gorham's key to becoming a well-rounded cook: "Go to the market, pick up something you've never seen before, read about it, then learn to cook it."

- **Never freak out.** "Even when we freak out, we don't let our freak-out show."

The Steakhouse, Resizzled

For their debut as a full-on restaurant in late 2009, Simpatica's Dyer, Owens, and new partner David Kreifels unveiled America's first indie steakhouse. Laurelhurst Market, a new kind of power spot, sizzles with affordable cuts, farm-connected ingredients, and a notable lack of cigar-chomping ambience. Greeting you at the door: pasture-raised meats and made-to-order sandwiches at a gleaming butcher counter. Judging by overnight lines, the formula hit a carnal nerve. Dyer calls it "a reaction to where the meat industry failed itself, a response to cutlets on foam trays wrapped in plastic with a diaper underneath." Any place that appeals to your dad *and* your eco-fretting friends is doing something right. In 2010, Laurelhurst Market shot to the top of *Bon Appétit*'s list of Best New Restaurants in America.

Laurelhurst Market sits at the stone entrance to the stately Laurelhurst neighborhood on East Burnside. Here Simpatica's comfort lords rehabbed an old mini-market

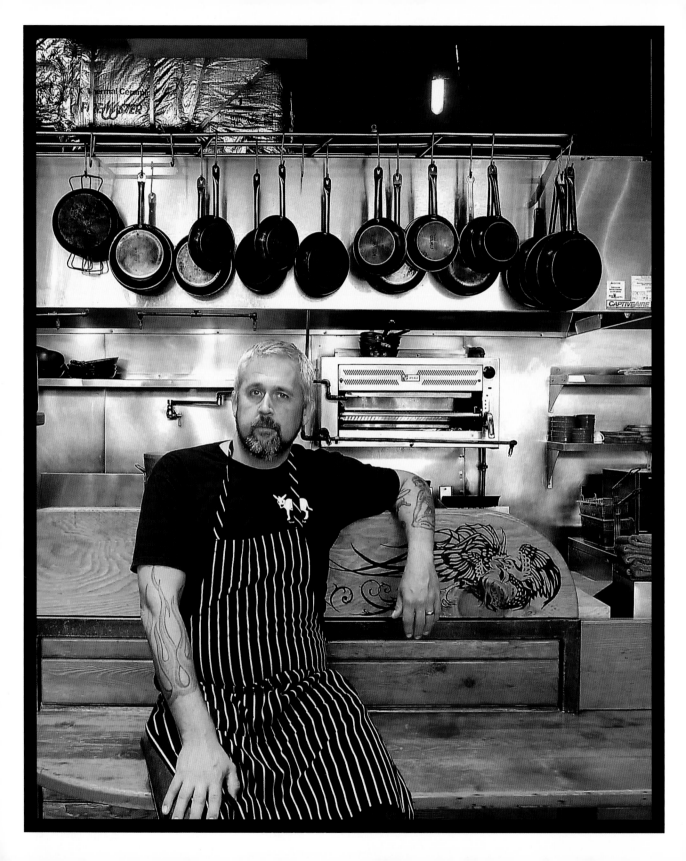

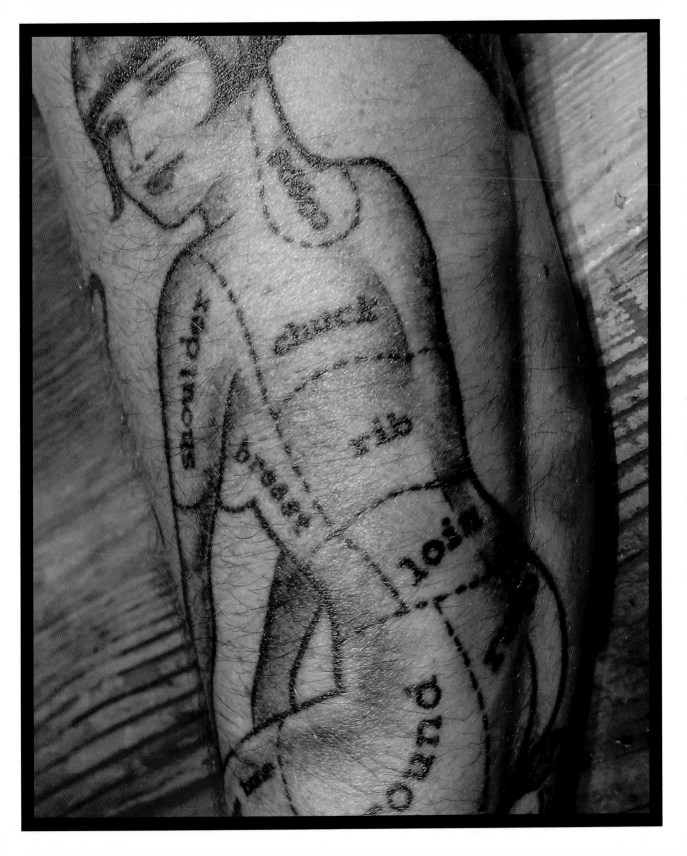

but kept the name. Now, Laurelhurst Market announces its ambitions on a chalkboard hanging over the clattering kitchen: a diagram of a cow outlining the night's cuts, snagged from the butcher counter steps away. A few high-end slabs are in the house, but the underdogs rule here: culotte, bavette, and other unsung parts prized for their flavor and friendly prices. Instead of relying on beef marbled like a Trump Tower lobby, the kitchen depends on juicy goodness, cooked-to-order execution, and the magic of brines, rubs, and smoke.

But steaks alone do not define the formula. Local pork chops—brick-size monsters doused in smoky bacon vinaigrette—stand like homages to bestial glory, and the twelve-hour brisket tees up with a wail of vinegar-punched barbecue sauce. The rethinking extends to a fresh breed of steakhouse sides, carrying cards of the season forged from comfort and whimsy: creamed chanterelles, roasted parsnips resting on fresh apple butter, mac 'n' cheese bubbling under a golden dome of crushed Northwest potato chips.

The butcher counter is the pinnacle of Laurelhurst Market, a modern caveman's larder stocked with handmade leaf lard, rendered duck fat, four kinds of smoked bacon, and a herd of buffalo wing sausages. "We won't be the cool kids forever," confesses Dyer. "In the end, we just want to be a good neighborhood place. That's what will sustain us."

Laurelhurst Market's Meaty Secrets

Grill tricks: Use briquettes to get the fire started, then add chunks of hardwood such as apple, pear, or pecan to add flavor and intensify the heat for a fine sear. Bank the coals to one side and check which direction the wind is blowing. Move the coals (or the grill) upwind of your meat. The wind helps push the heat and the smoke toward the food, allowing it to cook slowly and absorb as much flavor as possible.

The rosemary secret: Dunk fresh branches (or sprigs) in boiling water for about 10 seconds before using. This allows you to get the best out of rosemary, a key steak seasoning and popular "skewer" for meats. No more burning on the grill and no more harsh oils.

Favorite finishing rub: To season six steaks, blend fennel pollen (1 teaspoon), *piment d'Espellette* (2 teaspoons), and fine sea salt (2 teaspoons); rub on 1 minute before removing from the heat. Also great with lamb or grilled pork ribs, or just sprinkled over cut-up watermelon. Dyer calls it "sweet, salty, spicy, savory, and awesome."

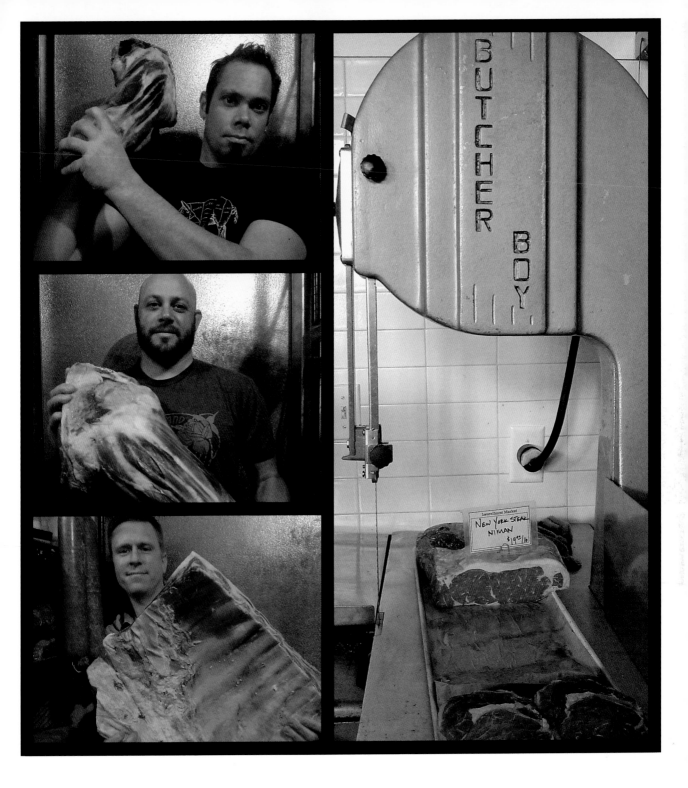

ROASTED SAUVIE ISLAND PARSNIPS WITH ORANGE-SAGE GREMOLATA

Laurelhurst Market's side dishes always carry a surprise. Here, it's a twist on *gremolata*, the traditional osso bucco condiment, with orange standing in for the classic lemon, and fresh sage in addition to the parsley. Sometimes the house smears fresh apple butter on the plate as a welcome mat for the roasted vegetables, transforming the dish into a celebration worthy of a holiday table.

Gremolata

1 tbsp finely chopped fresh sage

1 tbsp finely chopped fresh Italian parsley

½ tsp orange zest

1 garlic clove, finely chopped

Parsnips

2 tsp vegetable oil

5 medium parsnips, peeled and cut diagonally into 1-in-/2.5-cm-thick slices

2 small cipollini onions or medium shallots, peeled and quartered

Kosher salt and freshly ground black pepper

2 tbsp unsalted butter

1. FOR THE GREMOLATA: In a small bowl, combine the sage, parsley, orange zest, and garlic. Set aside.

2. TO MAKE THE PARSNIPS: Preheat the oven to 400°F/200°C/gas 6.

3. In a large ovenproof sauté pan, heat the vegetable oil over medium-high heat until a wisp of smoke appears. Immediately, add the parsnips, onions, and a pinch of salt and pepper. Without stirring, cook 2 minutes to brown the vegetables slightly. Turn them over to brown the other side and cook another minute or two. Remove from the heat and add the butter.

4. Transfer the pan to the oven and roast until the parsnips and onions are cooked through, about 10 minutes. Spoon the gremolata on top before serving.

SERVES 6

LAURELHURST MARKET'S MAC 'N' CHEESE WITH POTATO CHIP CRUST

Let's face it: Potato chips are a whole lot more fun than bread crumbs. When crushed over a fine mac 'n' cheese, they emerge as something beyond—a golden dome of glory, the epitome of crispy, salty, greasy, goodness. Attention to ingredients pays off: Use addictive extra-thick chips from Washington state's Tim's Cascade Chips, if you can find them, and torch-shaped Maccheroni al Torchio pasta, which encourages the sauce and cheese to invade its nooks and crannies. *Piment d'Espellette*, a mild ground chile powder from Spain's Basque region, is available in specialty shops, but cayenne can be substituted.

½ cup/115 g unsalted butter, softened

2 cups/480 ml whole milk

2 cups/480 ml heavy cream

2 bay leaves

4 fresh thyme sprigs

Kosher salt and freshly ground black pepper

1 medium onion, finely chopped

3 garlic cloves, peeled and slightly smashed

½ cup/60 g all-purpose flour

Freshly grated nutmeg

Pinch of *piment d'Espellette* or cayenne pepper

1 lb/455 g dry pasta shells

2 cups/225 g coarsely grated sharp Tillamook or other sharp Cheddar cheese

2 cups/225 g coarsely grated Gruyère cheese

1½ cups/70 g crushed Tim's Cascade Salted Potato Chips or other favorite thick-cut chips

1. Preheat the oven to 375°F/190°C/gas 5. Generously coat eight 6-oz/170-g ramekins or a 2-qt/2-L casserole with 1 tbsp of the butter.

2. In a small saucepan, warm the milk and cream over medium heat. Add the bay leaves, thyme, a pinch of salt, and a few grindings of pepper and bring to a simmer. Remove from the heat and set aside.

3. Bring a large pot of heavily salted water to a boil.

4. Meanwhile, in a medium saucepan, melt the remaining butter over medium heat. Stir in the onion, 1 tsp salt, and a few grindings of pepper. Sauté the onions until softened, 5 to 7 minutes. Add the garlic and cook, stirring often, until the onions are translucent, about 5 minutes. Add the flour in two batches, stirring continuously with a wooden spoon to make a roux. Cook, stirring and scraping the bottom of the pan to prevent browning, until the roux thickens, 4 to 5 minutes.

5. Strain the cream mixture, ½ cup/120 ml at a time, into the roux, whisking until smooth. Reduce the heat to low and add a few gratings of nutmeg, the *piment d'Espellette*, 1 tsp salt, and a few grindings of pepper. Simmer, whisking often, until thickened, about 30 minutes. Remove from the heat.

6. Cook the pasta in the pot of boiling water for a few minutes less than the directions on the package recommend. Drain well.

7. Meanwhile, in a blender, purée the cream mixture in batches until very smooth. Transfer to a large bowl. Stir in both cheeses and the drained pasta, mixing well. Transfer to the ramekins, overfilling them slightly, or to the casserole dish. Scatter the crushed potato chips evenly over the tops.

8. Place the ramekins or casserole on a baking sheet and bake until lightly browned and bubbling around the edges, about 35 minutes. If the chips brown too quickly, reduce the oven temperature a bit. Serve immediately.

SERVES 8

TASTY N SONS' CHEDDAR-BAKED APPLES WITH BACON LARDONS AND SPICED MAPLE SYRUP

While the pressure to eat something sensible builds throughout the day, a certain joy of capitulation rises with the dawn. So imagine a morning that begins with apple pie, but instead of a crust, a blanket of hot melted cheese, salty bits of bacon, and chile-spiked maple syrup.

Baked Apples

3 tbsp unsalted butter

2 tsp brown sugar

Pinch of ground cinnamon

Pinch of kosher salt

1 tsp lemon juice

4 large, firm apples, peeled, cored, and halved

8 oz/225 g cubed thick-cut, good-quality bacon

6 oz/170 g sharp Tillamook or other Cheddar cheese, thinly sliced

Spiced Maple Syrup

1 cup/235 ml pure maple syrup

1 tbsp minced jalapeño, seeds and membrane discarded

Pinch of cayenne pepper

Splash of lemon juice

1. TO MAKE THE BAKED APPLES: Preheat the oven to 325°F/165°C/gas 3. Line a baking sheet with foil.

2. In a small saucepan, melt the butter over medium heat. Remove from the heat and stir in the brown sugar, cinnamon, salt, and lemon juice. Place the apples in a large bowl and pour the butter mixture over them, tossing to evenly coat the fruit.

3. Place the apples, cut-side down, on the prepared baking sheet and bake until just cooked through, 8 to 10 minutes. Remove and set aside, but leave the oven on.

4. Meanwhile, in a medium skillet, slowly cook the bacon over medium-low heat, stirring occasionally, until cooked through, 7 to 10 minutes.

5. Turn the apples cut-side up and place a slice of cheese over each half. Return to the oven to melt the cheese, about 2 minutes.

6. TO MAKE THE SPICED MAPLE SYRUP: In a small saucepan, gently warm the maple syrup, jalapeño, and cayenne over medium-low heat. Remove from the heat and stir in the lemon juice.

7. Place two apple halves on each plate and top with one-fourth of the bacon bits. Spoon 1 to 2 tbsp of the warm maple syrup over the apples, letting it run down the sides and pool on the plate. Serve warm.

SERVES 4

TASTY BEEF JERKY

For handcrafted jerky inspiration, meat-master John Gorham heads to the Asian grocery for Chinese fried garlic and Golden Mountain Seasoning, a popular Thai sauce. The results? Just the right ratio of bounce and chew, sweet and spice. Partially freeze the beef to make slicing easier, or ask your butcher to do the trick. A home oven is fine for drying, or look for an inexpensive countertop dehydrator.

¾ cup/180 ml Golden Mountain Seasoning Sauce

½ cup/100 g firmly packed brown sugar

1 tbsp freshly squeezed lime juice

1 tbsp freshly ground black pepper

1 tbsp chile flakes

¼ cup/55 g Chinese fried garlic

One 2-lb/910-g beef eye of round, cut across the grain into thin slices and then into long strips

1. In a large bowl, stir together the seasoning sauce, brown sugar, lime juice, pepper, chile flakes, and garlic. Add the beef, and toss to coat well. Cover and refrigerate overnight. Toss again halfway through to coat all pieces well.

2. TO DRY MEAT IN A DEHYDRATOR: Preheat the dehydrator to 130°F/55°C. Place the meat slices, spacing them evenly without overlapping, on the trays. Dry in the dehydrator for 12 hours.

TO DRY IN THE OVEN: Preheat the oven to the "warm" setting or the lowest temperature possible. Arrange the meat slices in a single layer on parchment-lined baking sheets. Dry in the oven until the meat is completely dried, about 14 hours.

3. Store in a covered glass jar for up to 2 months.

MAKES ABOUT 1 LB/455 G

TASTY BLOODY MARY

When is a Bloody Mary more than a souped-up tomato juice with booze? When the glasses have rims of celery salt as wide as two-lane highways and long flaps of homemade beef jerky leap out of the top.

One 46-oz/1.4-L can tomato juice

½ cup/120 ml Worcestershire sauce

2½ tbsp freshly squeezed lemon juice

1 tbsp freshly squeezed lime juice, plus 1 lime, cut into 6 wedges

2 tsp Sriracha hot sauce

2 tsp freshly grated or favorite store-bought pure horseradish

1¾ tsp ground celery seed

½ cup/120 g kosher salt

¼ tsp freshly ground black pepper

¾ cup/180 ml vodka

One 6-oz/170-g jar pickled vegetables

Ice cubes

6 long celery stalks

6 pieces Tasty Beef Jerky (at left)

1. In a large pitcher, combine the tomato juice, Worcestershire, lemon juice, lime juice, Sriracha, and horseradish. Add ¼ tsp of the celery seed, 1 tsp of the salt, and the freshly ground pepper. Stir in the vodka. Spear the pickled vegetables onto long toothpicks and set aside.

2. In a wide, shallow bowl, combine the remaining 1½ tsp celery seed with the remaining salt. Rub the lime wedges around the rims of six tall glasses, moistening about ¾ in/2 cm all around. Quickly twirl the rims in the seasoned salt to create wide bands of celery salt.

3. Fill each glass three-quarters full with ice. Stir the mix well and pour over the ice. Garnish each with a celery stick and a piece of beef jerky, making sure they poke a couple of inches out of the glass. Garnish with the speared pickled vegetables and serve.

MAKES 6 COCKTAILS

DAVID BRIGGS
XOCOLATL DE DAVID

A self-taught food artist puts the squeal in chocolates.

David Briggs hunts for chocolate ideas with the dogged intensity of Tom Hanks crawling through cinematic battlefields to find Private Ryan. His playbook includes chocolate corn milk, chocolate roux, and chocolate fruit preserves made with anything dropping off an Oregon tree. His exploration of chocolate and charcuterie comes to fruition in a $20 crock of Foitella, a chocolate foie gras spread meant for slathering over baguettes or, even better, vanilla wafers. "It's like a foie gras Milano," says Briggs, giggling at the thought.

But his real genius is reimagining the American candy bar. The Raleigh Bar, a signature in his Xocolatl de David collection, is the thinking person's Snickers. Each flavor pops with pecan nougat, a layer of caramel smoky enough to set off alarms, and a thin glaze of dark chocolate, almost black in its austere intensity. So far, Raleigh Bars come three ways: plain, bourbon-spiked, or, the cult favorite, with bacon—not bacon bits, mind you, just pure porky flavor mainlined right into the caramel. One bite, and there's no going back. *Bon Appétit*'s Andrew Knowlton couldn't resist, calling the Raleigh "the best chocolate candy I've had."

In Briggs's hands, chocolate, crunch, pork, salt, and heat crash together into something bold and new. His Chicharrón Bar is a kind of possessed Nestlé Crunch, crackling with homemade fried pork rinds, dark Bolivian chocolate, salt from a stash of crystalline possibilities, and locally grown *aji dulce* chile peppers. Chocolate rarely offers the primal punch of pig's skin or commands a waiting list, as this one does. But Briggs is not going for shock value: "For hundreds of years, other cultures have been bringing chocolate into meat. I'm just flipping it, bringing meat into chocolate."

The squeals are just beginning. Yelled the editors of *Sunset* magazine, "We're obsessing over the Raleigh Bars." They're not alone.

Raising the Bars

Briggs is the embodiment of Portland's food dream: a guy who dropped everything at age thirty to become a chocolatier, fearlessly, without a sugar daddy in the wings. In 2006, he was line cooking and butchering his way through Portland's celebrated Park Kitchen when he saw his future: a dead end in a small kitchen where the top slots were locked down. In his spare time, he played with chocolates, and he soon found himself on the ground floor of

the chocolate-bacon craze. A growing reputation led to wild chocolate dinners and a loyal following for bonbons sold at Steve Jones's Cheese Bar, a beacon of artisanal food trends. Briggs even had a free marketing campaign: To throw down support, Park Kitchen included a Xocolatl de David with every check.

In 2009 he rolled the dice on his own, renting kitchen space to feed online sales and growing orders. This is not Willy Wonka's factory. Briggs works in a storage room and ad hoc office for the cult sandwich shop Meat Cheese Bread in Southeast. He's a one-man factory, hand-dipping and wrapping each chocolate while sharing air space with stacks of Boylan's soda and an old Atari Roadblaster arcade. But the economics work. At $200, rent is cheap, so money is invested in quality ingredients not typically found in a chocolatier's closet: single-origin chocolates and artisan salts, for sure, but also local goat cheese, wild plums, and hand-cured meats. In a few short years, Xocolatl de David's sales have zoomed from $500 to $50,000, as local chefs and shop owners have helped get the word out. That's how it works here: Everyone celebrates and champions each other. Zero sum game does not apply in Portland.

When Pig's Blood Chocolates Fly

Pig's blood chocolates look like one of the nice chocolates snuggled in a box of See's Candies, except for the smoked Spanish paprika on top, which could be mistaken for dried blood. But that's the point, says Briggs, who caught inspiration one night while eating Blood Noodles at Le Pigeon. Now he makes the hand-dipped squares twice a year, religiously, for Halloween and Valentine's Day. What does pig's blood do for these elegant truffles? To believers, the blood infuses the ganache with a subtle iron flavor, like spinach but much better. But only die-hard customers know for sure. Confesses Briggs: "I end up giving most of them away, but I love making them anyway."

New ideas are rolling. A bar starring Benton's Smoked Mountain Country Ham is in the works, and Briggs is furiously putting the finishing touches on a "caviar bar" surfaced with glistening beads of charred bamboo salt. "It's all salty chocolate up front," he explains, and "then it blooms on the taste buds, and you get that 'Oh wow, it's *caviar*' moment."

David's Meaty Chocolate Cabinet

Think of chocolate as a food, not a sweet. That's the Briggs philosophy in a nutshell. He keeps the following on his shelf of adventure:

Single-origin chocolates—Briggs calls chocolates from one region or one farm "more nuanced and more interesting than the blended varieties." Favorite brand: Felchlin's 68 percent Bolivian chocolate, "deep but understated and perfect for baking or experiments."

Smoked bacon—"Bacon lifts out the savory side of chocolate, but only a smoky bacon can make magic happen."

Finishing salts and sea salts—Briggs's motto: "A final sprinkle of fleur de sel (briny, crunchy salt) will make any chocolate dessert better." For a big statement, he searches The Meadow, a prime resource for salt exotica headquartered in Portland. Recent finds include smoky, amber-colored Halen Mon Gold flakes from Wales and Amabito No Mooshio, a Japanese sea salt that "shouts deep umami flavor."

Charcuterie—"Chocolate and cured meats are amazing together. I love to serve a block of chocolate on a tray with chorizo, finocciona, and pancetta, then let everyone shave their own on top."

CHORIZO XOCOLATL SANDWICH

When challenged to create a sandwich for this book, David Briggs juggled three of his favorite chocolate combos into one new idea: chocolate and chorizo; chocolate and olive oil; chocolate and sherry vinegar. The arugula's sharp peppery bite helps cut through the richness.

Chocolate Spread

½ tsp sugar

1 tsp natural cocoa powder (not Dutch processed)

¼ tsp Pomona's Natural Pectin

¼ cup plus 2 tbsp/90 ml heavy cream

5 oz/140 g dark chocolate, 70% cocoa, coarsely chopped

Pinch of fleur de sel

2 tbsp extra-virgin olive oil

½ tsp sherry vinegar

Pinch of fleur de sel

2 oz/55 g arugula

1 baguette, cut crosswise into 4 equal sections

2 to 3 oz/55 to 85 g dry-cured chorizo, cut diagonally into ¼-in-/6-mm-thick slices

1. TO MAKE THE CHOCOLATE SPREAD: In a medium bowl, combine the sugar, cocoa powder, and pectin. In a small saucepan, bring the cream to a full boil over medium-high heat. Remove from the heat immediately. Pour the cream into the sugar mixture and whisk vigorously until smooth. Using a rubber spatula, stir in the chocolate. Continue to stir vigorously for a few minutes, until the mixture resembles a thick pudding. Stir in the fleur de sel. Cool at room temperature for 2 hours.

2. Preheat the broiler. In a medium bowl, whisk 1 tsp of the olive oil with the vinegar and fleur de sel. Add the arugula and gently toss.

3. Cut each baguette section in half horizontally but not all the way through. On a baking sheet, open the bread sections and brush the insides with the remaining olive oil. Toast the bread, open faced, under the broiler for 30 seconds, or until golden brown. Spread 1 tbsp of the chocolate mixture on each side of the bread. Arrange a single layer of chorizo and a handful of arugula over one half and close the two halves together. Transfer to plates and serve.

SERVES 4

CHAPTER 2
LOCAL HEROES

Four chefs reset the homegrown
table with strange beauty and
extreme pleasures.

FROSTY'S
· ONE OF A KIND ·
7 DIFFERENT CHILES
CHILE FLAKE
IT'S
SMOKIN' $3.00
HOT (2 oz.)

Grass-pastured TURKEY

Holiday Grass Pastured

Happy turkeys, Happy People,
Celebrate Thanksgiving!!
Celebrate Life!!!

HOLIDAY GRASS PASTURED HERITAGE TURKEYS

JOHN TABOADA

NAVARRE

A free-thinker bucks Big Ag with a mountain of broccoli rabe.

"More God-damn squash," says John Taboada surveying his battlefield one September morning, knowing the fight ahead. Instead of a heavenly harvest, the fall of 2010 brought an early season of bone-chilling rain and suicide-gray skies, transforming one of the country's most prolific farm scenes into a mixed grocery bag. But the show must go on at his thirty-seat Navarre, where every hand-forged table and rickety stool is piled with just-picked produce by eight in the morning, while cooks hatch strategies on the spot. A handsome battalion of leaf-topped beets, violet-colored pea pods, and cabbages the size of bowling balls await their future in mason jars, pickle baths, and roasting pans. But bins of malnourished fennel and cracked heirloom tomatoes must also be accounted for, along with bushels of kale and mounds of squash. Nothing will be thrown away, not even stems. That's the overriding philosophy here. Everything must be quickly preserved or processed in a kitchen the size of Thomas Keller's hall closet.

In a city that prides itself on local and sustainable, no place embraces the mind-set more completely than Navarre, Portland's anticorporate headquarters since 2001. Taboada lives and dies with the fortunes of one urban farm in Southeast Portland, practically a stone's throw from his front door. Navarre has opted into an alternative food economy called community-supported agriculture (CSA). In this system, a community of individuals act as shareholders in a small, quality-focused farm, and, in return, they receive weekly deliveries of what the farm produces.

Taboada's commitment to buy one-tenth of the crop at the 47th Avenue Farm, come hell or high water, means he shares in the risks and the rewards of farm life. If a snowstorm wipes out the fields, as it did one year, the kitchen manages without the lovely spring greens brightening the menus of Navarre's competitors. No cheating and no cherry picking from other suppliers; that would violate Taboada's self-imposed rule. He toughs it out for months if necessary, relying on mountains of broccoli rabe and whatever else is Darwinian enough to crawl out of the ground and through his door. But when the sun shines mightily, few restaurants boast sweeter carrots or more angelic cauliflower.

Interestingly, Navarre never knows what the farm will deliver, so you never know what will be on the menu. It just depends on whatever the kitchen is fixating over at the

moment. You might stumble on five gratins, all amazing, or in deep summer, the juiciest tomatoes ever, served ten different ways, from cakes to condiments. Or you might find yourself in the midst of Taboada's quest to nail the perfect pâté (he did it) or his two-year argument with Renato the waiter over the correct technique for polenta (he lost).

The key to Navarre's psyche lies in its elaborate menu system, a mysterious collection of lists and sublists, each driven by a different philosophy. To begin, everyone is handed a pencil and what looks like a sushi menu, with options that introduce themselves as only "bird" or "lamb." These dishes are Navarre's analog to sit-com regulars—a cast of nonseasonal staples often starring the kitchen's butchery skills. Your job is to check off whatever appeals. Meanwhile, printed nightly specials showcase the CSA-driven "make-do" mentality with unusual pairings of fruits and vegetables born from the kitchen's seasonal logic. When you taste the sweet double dare of roasted beets and fresh cherries, or the unexpected juice and crunch of raw peaches and tomatoes, it all seems so brilliant, so obvious. Like everything at Navarre, these dishes stand on their own merits, free of sauces, presentation, and even garnishes.

Yet another list, handwritten on a hanging mirror, represents scholarly incursions into a specific cuisine and culture, perhaps Burgundy or Basque territory, changing every few months with dozens of options and rigorous hunts for matching wines (itself a subdivision of an adventurous house list serving fifty options by the glass based solely on "wines we like"). For Taboada, it's about staying as true as possible to the techniques and attitudes of whatever region he has adopted. But then, 47th Avenue's "Farmer Laura" drops off ten tubs of broccoli rabe . . . and his romantic ideas are shaken to his core. How does broccoli rabe fit with his lovely specials from the Loire Valley?

Every week Taboada wonders why he set up the restaurant this way. "I can get really emotional and overwhelmed by what walks in the door," he admits. "But once I calm down, focus, and figure out what to do, I'm grounded again."

Embracing Inconsistency

Navarre's ad hoc supply-chain system has meant giving up notions Taboada once held dear: perfection, choice, pushing the edge of flavor. Now, instead of demanding vegetables at their peak, he confronts entire life cycles, altering dishes as an ingredient evolves in the field from mild to sweet to bitter to dead, making appearances on his watch during each phase. That means you might find yourself staring at candied fennel stems, weird little pickles, or root vegetables roasted with a gnarly realism, scary roots and all. Any given dish can be ugly, joyful, sublimely simple, or simply unforgettable, and often all at once. It's the wild beauty of how this place works. "Everyone said we needed to be more consistent, but I let that go," says the shaggy-haired chef. "I'm embracing inconsistency. We are driven by how much things *change*. If you try to fight it, you lose. It's all bigger than you, bigger than the CSA. It's the weather. The farm is not consistent. If you want consistency, go to Applebee's."

Navarre by the Numbers

Recipes conjured during the past two years: **2,730**

Number of house pâtés: **50**

Variations on broccoli rabe: **45**

Don't call us a restaurant.

John Tabaoda was way ahead of the curve when he pioneered Portland's garage gourmet scene on the blue-collar east side. He crafted the interior, down to the spare white-oak tables, from a tree in his parents' Maryland backyard, and then filled it with the best ingredients, a local food gestalt, and his own definition of how a restaurant could be run—alive, responding to the moment, with a different way of ordering, which implied a different way of behaving.

Right from the beginning he was adamant that no one call it a *restaurant*. The word itself carried expectations. He simply calls Navarre an "eat spot."

It's an apt description of a place that is many things—a moody French roadhouse, a food lovers' mini-mart, and a monument to the home-canning movement—all run by a charismatic guy who sometimes cooks, sometimes hosts, and always looks like he just rolled out of bed. Taboada built this intimate sanctuary as much for customers to soak in good conversation as for them to enjoy good food. He lives to provide the tools for a night of magic. That's why he never reveals his CSA program or explains his multiple menu schemes to customers. That would be posturing, a marketing ploy, "noise" as he calls it, stuff that would get in the way of the experience. "Ultimately, it's about the table," says Taboada. "Everything happens there, including the realization that four hours later you've revealed forgotten childhood secrets—not just to dining companions but to yourself."

The Gospel According to John Taboada

Navarre's leaf-to-stem approach drives on three central truths of the kitchen, as laid down here:

Braise the greens—"We cook them to death, like a slow-roasted piece of meat cooked to the bone. And always in a pot of water mixed with changing vinegars to bring out the sweetness."

Roast the vegetables—"I roast them at 400 or 500°F until they burn on the edges. The heat helps drive out the natural sugar. It's like cooking over fire."

Pickle everything—"We only pickle in vinegar water. The idea is to keep the pickle as close to the original vegetable, fruit, or mushroom. We use pickles as ingredients, not condiments. They're necessary to our system, not a luxury."

Parting Words

"All this intellectual stuff and theory is fine, but in the end, I tell my cooks, 'Just make it taste good.'"

HEIRLOOM TOMATOES AND PEACHES

Like many combos at Navarre, this one seems strange until you taste it—and then the sky opens: stars shooting, juice squirting. Imagine a Caprese salad but better—fruity *and* vegetal and fortified with grassy basil. It's the fleeting profundity of late summer in one bite.

1½ tsp aged balsamic vinegar

Fine sea salt

2 large ripe heirloom tomatoes, cored and cut into ½-in/12-mm cubes

1 large ripe peach, pit removed and cut into thin wedges

20 fresh basil leaves, stemmed and coarsely chopped

1 tbsp extra-virgin olive oil

Freshly ground black pepper

In a small bowl, combine the vinegar and ½ tsp salt. In a large bowl, combine the tomatoes, peach, and basil leaves. Drizzle the olive oil and vinegar-salt mixture over the top. Toss gently with your hands and season with salt and pepper. Serve immediately.

SERVES 4 TO 6

ROASTED BEET GREENS WITH GRUYÈRE

This simple dish is classic Navarre: rooty greens roasted until just crisp and celebrating their elemental realism with just enough input from a little salt and a punch of aged Gruyère cheese.

12 oz/280 g tender beet greens, stemmed and coarsely chopped

1 tbsp vegetable oil

½ tsp fine sea salt

¾ cup/85 g grated cave-aged Gruyère

1. Preheat the oven to 400°F/200°C/gas 6.

2. Place a baking sheet in the oven for 5 minutes. In a large bowl, toss the beet greens with the vegetable oil and salt. The greens should be coated lightly and glistening.

3. Spread the greens evenly over the hot baking sheet, fluffing them up a bit. Sprinkle the cheese in a light layer over the greens. Roast until the cheese melts and the greens are just wilted, about 8 minutes. Serve immediately.

SERVES 6

POLENTA WITH CANDIED BEETS, FRESH CHERRIES, AND PICKLED PORCINI

The seven-course Stumptown Coffee Pairing Dinner at Navarre was a grand experiment, and in the summer of 2006 it expanded tongues and minds. "The rules have been made for wine dinners," remarked chef John Taboada back then. "We have no frame of reference for this kind of pairing." After weeks engulfed in coffee vapors and recipe testing, Taboada and Stumptown founder Duane Sorensen unveiled their vision, as fresh-roasted Panama Esmeralda Reserve, the Cristal champagne of coffee, danced alongside fantastic goose rillettes and licorice-y *pan d'epices* bread. The peak moment? Sipping the aptly named Nicaragua Los Delirios while digging into polenta bearing the sweetest beets, the smell of the cherry tree, the taste of the forest. You can candy the beets in advance. Just be sure to "cook them to death," as Taboada says, to develop the sugars, and keep the greens for roasting (see page 61).

Candied Beets

5 medium beets, stemmed

1 cup/240 g sugar

Juice and zest of 1 lemon

1 juniper berry

Polenta

Fine sea salt

2 cups/320 g good-quality polenta

2 tbsp unsalted butter

10 oz/280 g fresh cherries, stemmed

½ cup/115 g thinly sliced Navarre's Pickled Porcini (page 64)

1 tbsp porcini oil or hazelnut oil for drizzling

½ lemon

Freshly ground black pepper

1. TO MAKE THE CANDIED BEETS: Preheat the oven to 350°F/180°C/gas 4.

2. Place the whole beets in a baking dish, add enough water to reach ¼ in/6 mm up from the bottom of the pan, then cover tightly with foil. Bake until the beets are fork-tender and very sweet, at least 50 minutes but ideally up to 3 hours. (If cooking more than 50 minutes, check water level and replenish if needed.) Cool for 30 minutes. While still warm, rub your fingers over the skins to remove. Cut into ½-in/12-mm cubes. You will have about 2 cups.

3. In a medium saucepan over medium heat, combine the sugar and 3½ cups/840 ml water. Bring to a boil, stirring to dissolve the sugar. Add the beets, lemon juice, and juniper berry. Simmer over low heat, until the liquid reduces to a thick syrup and the beets are slightly transparent and almost glowing, about 4 hours. Check the water over time, adding small amounts as needed. Stir in the lemon zest. Remove from the heat and store the beets in the liquid until ready to use. (They will keep for up to 1 month in the refrigerator.)

4. TO MAKE THE POLENTA: In a medium pot over high heat, bring 5 cups/1.2 L water to a boil. Reduce the heat to medium and add 2 tsp salt. Slowly add the polenta in a thin stream, stirring constantly with a wooden spoon, always in one direction—a technique learned from Renato the waiter—until all the polenta is incorporated. Cook until the polenta gets harder to stir and "drinks" up the liquid, 15 to 20 minutes. Add 1 cup/240 ml water. Continue cooking for another hour or more, adding water as needed (up to 10 cups/2.4 L total), stirring and scraping the bottom of the pan frequently as the polenta gently bubbles and thickens. When finished, it will have the consistency of a buttercream frosting or properly mixed mortar. Stir in the butter and season with salt. Pour the polenta onto a large cutting board or clean flat surface. Use a spatula to draw it up from the sides onto itself to form a dome. Cover with a damp towel and let rest for 10 minutes.

5. Over a small bowl, pit the cherries and tear the fruit into quarters, letting them fall into their own juice. Cut the polenta into 1/3-in-/8-mm-thick slices and transfer to warm plates. (Cover and refrigerate leftover polenta for up to 3 days.) Top each slice with a spoonful of cherries and juice, and a spoonful of candied beets. Sprinkle each serving with a few of the pickled porcini slices and drizzle with a little porcini oil. Finish with a squeeze of lemon juice and freshly ground black pepper before serving.

SERVES 6 TO 8

NAVARRE'S
PICKLED PORCINI

The longer these earthy gems sit in olive oil (3 to 6 months is ideal) the richer the rewards. Another bonus: a porcini-infused oil for drizzling on just about anything—pasta, polenta, omelets, or steak. Cooks in the fast lane can opt for the quicker of two versions here. Eat the mushrooms like pickles, add slices to salads, or toss with braised chicken.

1 lb/455 kg fresh medium porcini

3 cups/720 ml muscatel or sweet aged wine vinegar

1 fresh thyme sprig

1 tbsp fine sea salt

About 3 cups/720 ml high-quality extra-virgin olive oil (optional)

1. Wipe the grit from the porcini with a damp towel. Cut them into quarters or halves about the size of your thumb. (For larger porcini, cut into sixths or eighths.)

2. In a medium saucepan, bring the vinegar to a boil over high heat. Lower the heat to a simmer and stir in the mushrooms, thyme, and salt. Cook until the mushrooms are just tender, 8 to 10 minutes. Let cool completely in the vinegar.

3. FOR A QUICK PICKLE: Transfer the mushrooms and liquid to a glass container, cover, and refrigerate for 24 hours. Strain the mushrooms, reserving the vinegar to use in salads or other dishes.

FOR A SLOW PICKLE (AND PORCINI OIL): Transfer the mushrooms and liquid to a glass container, cover, and refrigerate for 3 days. Strain the mushrooms, saving the vinegar to use in salads or other dishes. Transfer the mushrooms to a 1-qt/960-ml sanitized jar. In a small saucepan, gently warm the olive oil over low heat. Pour the warm oil into the jar to cover the mushrooms, and process according to USDA canning standards. (The oil should cover the mushrooms completely; if not, add more oil.) Store in a dark, cool cabinet for 3 to 6 months. After opening, store in the refrigerator. Before serving, allow the oil to come to room temperature.

MAKES ABOUT 1 QT/960 ML

HALIBUT BAKED WITH AÏOLI

This Navarre signature takes inspiration from Oregon's coast and chef John Taboada's Spanish roots. Think seared, super-moist halibut emerging from the oven under a "soufflé" of garlic mayonnaise, the essence of creamy goodness. The ingredients are simple, but the trick is in the timing: lightly browning the aïoli without overcooking the fish. Get it right, and it's magic.

Aïoli

4 garlic cloves

Fine sea salt

1 tsp muscatel vinegar

1/4 tsp Dijon mustard

1 egg yolk

1 cup/240 ml vegetable oil

Fish

2 tsp vegetable oil

1 1/2 tsp fine sea salt

Six 6-oz/170-g halibut fillets, each 1 in/2.5 cm thick, skin removed

1. TO MAKE THE AÏOLI: Using a mortar and pestle, pound the garlic and 1/2 tsp salt to a paste. Transfer to a glass or stainless-steel (i.e., nonreactive) bowl if necessary. Whisk in the vinegar, mustard, and egg yolk. Very slowly drizzle in the vegetable oil, 1 tsp at a time, whisking constantly. Continue adding the oil slowly, whisking until thick and emulsified. Add the remaining oil in a fine stream, whisking until smooth and glossy. Season with salt. Use within 1 hour, or cover and refrigerate for up to 2 days.

2. TO COOK THE FISH: Preheat the oven to 350°F/180°C/gas 4. Rub the vegetable oil and salt over the halibut.

3. Preheat two large, ovenproof skillets (or if you have only one large skillet, cook in two batches) over medium-high heat until very hot. Sear the halibut for about 3 minutes, and then carefully flip over. Top each fillet with a 1/2-in-/12-mm-thick dollop of aïoli and immediately transfer to the oven. Roast until the fish is just cooked through and the aïoli is slightly puffed and golden brown, 3 to 4 minutes. (Watch carefully so that you don't overcook the fish; it can dry out very quickly.) When a fork easily passes through the center without resistance, the fish is ready. Serve immediately.

SERVES 6

MATT LIGHTNER
CASTAGNA

A foraging chef finds a new Oregon cuisine, and it's wild in every way imaginable.

Unlike Portland's self-taught rebel chefs, Castagna's Matt Lightner trained at two top foodie think tanks. At Spain's Mugaritz, in a swift climb from unpaid student to sous chef, he perfected the art of edible landscapes inspired by nearby locales and science kits. At Copenhagen's Noma, he gleaned the new hypernatural philosophy at the center of today's most advanced food conversation. By age twenty-eight, he possessed technical skills, experience, and ideas matched by only a dozen or so chefs in America. He was also out of a job.

When his visa expired in 2009, Lightner flew back to the States only to find America's crumbled restaurant world. In Chicago, modernist dining rooms once crawling with bloggerati looked like ghost ships. No one was hiring. In New York's top spots, he couldn't even find work as a "stage" or unpaid kitchen hand. Lightner had no money and no prospects, just a sister in Portland and possibilities in a place he once called home. When he wheeled back into Stumptown with all his possessions in a beat-up Chrysler, Matt Lightner, son of Nebraska, wasn't planning a coup of Oregon cuisine; he was just swimming upriver to survive, like every other chef in a cooked economy, and wondering if the sequel to his avant-garde training would translate to a waiter's job.

He found luck and an opening at Castagna, a respected wallflower serving the same Italian-French menu for ten years running on busy Southeast Hawthorne. Meeting Lightner, owner Monique Siu did more than replace her departing chef. With the economy throwing jeers at fine dining and Portland's celebrated scene reveling in food carts, she gambled on an unknown chef with super-challenging ideas in wallet-quivering times. Lightner planted the seeds for his far-out experiments right on the sidewalk. Every night thereafter, he ducked out his kitchen door to pluck day lilies and cyprus and other curious botanicals from a Garden of Eden staring down a tattoo art gallery across the street. In Lightner's world, every location is ripe for picking, even a busy street corner next to a bus stop.

That's the beauty of what he brings to Portland's table, an uprooting of ideas. Lightner forages backyards and turns over stones, literally, to redraw the boundaries of taste and place. Imagine James Beard returning, but as a hiker and abstract expressionist driven to celebrate not just the seasons but every bark and stem in dishes constructed like architect Frank Gehry's wild and wavy walls.

No two dishes are alike, but each tells a story with visual drama and characters sniffed out on riverbanks or swept off the forest floor. Over the course of a meal, you might encounter the super-sour surprise of wood sorrel or meet wild lady fern fronds toasted into crisp curlicues to cap a drift of smoked buttermilk and a boulder of lamb as grunt-worthy as central Texas barbecue. When fried morels stuffed with hot rabbit sausage, resting on wet, robust nettle leaves and releasing the earthy steam of pine nut gravy, arrive on a jet-black stone, we, the fine diners, are suddenly out there with him, hiking in muddy boots or sitting under a giant Douglas fir tree.

On his days off, Lightner surveys the Oregon coast, tide charts in hand, waiting for the right moment to snatch up sea lettuce, which he transforms into a briny broth that goes straight to the brain. He reaches deep into herbs, roots, and vegetables to help us understand the beauty; even a weed, something we step on, is ennobled. Lightner is looking under things, and when you realize this, his otherworldly food—which doesn't look like food at all—opens up. Something hides beneath the surface of every dish, just as in nature, where mushrooms sprout under mossy logs and wild greens burrow under snow. In Lightner's territory, the eater becomes the explorer.

Science helps him get there, but Lightner's pursuit is cooking, not molecular gastronomy. There's no pretension, no shock and awe, no hocus-pocus. This is not José Andrés's foie gras cotton candy or Alinea's trapeze-swinging bacon. Lightner is concerned with the primacy of ingredients and the finished product—a point that modernist cooking often misses. This is real food, a serious, satisfying *meal*—eye-popping for sure but grounded and crafted to the max.

What Lightner is doing is so different that it's pointless to describe him alongside other Oregon chefs. He's a storyteller, tracking a place for himself among the region's iconic imagists: writer Ken Kesey; landscape painter James Lavadour, an abstract artist of searing emotion; even the band of world-music pioneers called Oregon, who inspired astronauts to take their soundtrack straight to the moon. It's the Northwest experience but told through plates.

Best Matt Lightner Invention

Wild ginger ice cream sundae. Is it dessert? Japanese ikebana? Or just a crazy soft serve swirl holding giant knobs of candied rhubarb, like great gummy bears from the sky, and crisp-baked gingerbread shards to channel broken ice cream cones? Maybe it's the salad you *wish* your mother served: a plate of ice cream sprouting nine botanicals on top, each bearing a singular flavor, making every bite a different experience. Does it matter?

Delights and Prejudices

In his ever-present Kansas City Chiefs jersey and Vans sneakers, Lightner doesn't look like a revolutionary. He may be an army of one, but his challenge to the "local and seasonal" status quo is refreshing. He's not shy about pronouncing the farm-to-table movement dead: "It's just a genre. Everyone gets stuff from a farm. Don't know anyone who doesn't."

At least he's asking the questions: Who are we? What defines *this* place, *our* soul? What is the next salmon?

Some answers arrive at Castagna like a ritualistic Japanese *kaiseki* meal, unfolding in kaleidoscopic fashion on a procession of river rocks, bark, and bone-colored plates that cascade before you as if in a silent movie while colors ravish the eye. The journey often begins with a small wooden box holding rough stones and origami folds of purple carrot leather and glossy violet gel, conjuring exotic butterflies alighting in a stream.

The kitchen's radical transformation has eluded Castagna's old-guard staff. No one seems to notice that the famed steak and haystack fries have been replaced by halibut cloaked like a Christo installation in an outsized cabbage leaf. Waiters casually drop off a menu that might as well be a page from the Talmud or the Dead Sea Scrolls, leaving diners to divine the meaning of "sunchoke with sunflower and apple," then returning with a cheery "Are you ready to order?" The experience is like finding a Picasso in an auto body shop.

Yet, this is also Castagna's charm, serving the apex of cuisine out of time and place in a working-class neighborhood open to anyone, even a dude in a lumberjack shirt. The low cost of admission for this cooking—$65 for four courses and a wonderment of gratis amusements from the kitchen—is unheard of, anywhere. Monique Siu has remade ambition on a small, exciting scale, showing that destination dining can live outside of exclusive wallets.

It couldn't last. And it didn't.

In the summer of 2011, New York came knocking. Lightner wasn't looking to leave Oregon. He won't find edible ferns growing out of Manhattan's manhole covers. But the offer from power-broking food lover Jodi Richard was too great to pass up: triple the salary, health care, and the ability to think big. Atera, his new Tribeca restaurant, opened in early 2012 with eighteen seats—*seats!*—and a $500,000 dream kitchen of his own design.

It's a long drive from Hawthorne Boulevard.

The Manhattan Project

Now begins a new chapter for Portland, too. Since Lightner's departure, being part of the modernist—and global—dialogue has new urgency in a city that embraces isolationism. High-end dining is a hard sell in Stumptown; even as accolades piled up, Lightner often cooked to half-empty dining rooms. But Sui is not deterred, declaring "We cannot just go back to being who we were." She handed the kitchen keys to Lightner's understudy, Justin Woodward, a pastry alum of New York's famed modernist lab W-D 50. Clearly, he's an artist in bloom and maybe a dessert genius in the making. Just don't tell New York.

For Lightner, The Big Apple is just the next frontier. He refuses to label his style, committing only to "exploring a new definition of American cooking, to dig deeper, to see where that leads." Creating a nature-based cuisine in a cement city will be challenging. But Lightner, once a competitive bowler, is up to the task; on a good night, he can still lay down a cool 256 in the lanes. Already, he's combing the wilds of the Northeast, continuing his search for the hidden and the forgotten while making art and sense of it. Oregon's forest was the ground floor; the sky is clearly the limit for this unstoppable force.

Atera is Lightner's R&D lab, with $150 tasting menus and plans for a separate kitchen where customers can watch how farming, foraging, science, and imagination might collaborate in a modernist fashion. Mostly, he and Richard are test-driving ideas for a long-term project, a destination restaurant that could land anywhere in the world. Maybe even in Oregon.

For now, Lightner carries Spain's surrealism and Copenhagen's naturalism in his back pocket. But, to survive the test of New York, he may need the ace up his sleeve, Portland attitude: "I'm just going with my own style. I'm finding my own path. If people don't like it, fine. If it doesn't work out, it doesn't work out."

Best Matt Lightner Advice

Grow, pluck, and taste. "Herbs and flowers add elements of surprise, but I use them to gain a deep savor in place of cream and butter. We tend to use herbs only in places we've seen them before. Basil is always with pasta, but it goes with a million things—pears, pistachios, even lamb brings out that licorice tone, that potency. First taste the herb on its own, and then think: What would that flavor pair with? Dill is a favorite. I love it with sweet things. Dill pollen is very sweet; sprinkle it over meats, fish, or fruit. I rub geranium leaves over lamb or duck before grilling for a beautiful perfume. It's about playing and expanding possibility."

SALSIFY IMPERSONATING FOREST LOGS

Matt Lightner suggests an alternative storyline to the usual roasted vegetable side, told with a crisscross of long brown salsify roots (an artichoke-like member of the daisy family) soaked in sweet, fleshy wild licorice and honey, then rolled in teeny leaves and woodlike shavings of toasted hazelnuts. Are they fallen logs in a mossy forest or a reminder of Oregon's logging history? Or just licorice-sharp vegetable sticks that pair brilliantly with charred meat and nuts? You decide. Get in the spirit and hunt for hard-to-find roots at farmers' markets or online, or use the easy alternatives.

3 qt/2.8 L water

10 fresh wild licorice roots or 1 tbsp anise seeds

4 juniper berries

1 tsp fennel seeds

½ cup/170 ml honey, plus 1 tsp

1½ tsp fine sea salt

1 cup plus 3 tbsp/165 g chestnut flour

10 to 12 salsify or 6 parsnips, peeled and cut into 5-in-/12-cm-long pieces

¾ cup/100 g raw hazelnuts, with skin

5 sprigs fresh parsley, stemmed and finely chopped

5 sprigs fresh fennel fronds, stemmed and finely chopped

5 sprigs fresh tarragon, stemmed and finely chopped

3 tbsp unsalted butter

10 sprigs dill

10 fresh chives, cut into 2-in/5-cm pieces

1. Preheat the oven to 250°F/120°C/gas ½.

2. In a small saucepan, combine the water, licorice roots, juniper berries, fennel seeds, ½ cup/170 ml honey, and 1 tsp of the salt. Bring to a boil and immediately turn off the heat. Infuse at room temperature until fragrant, about 1 hour.

3. Meanwhile, spread the chestnut flour on a baking sheet and toast in the oven until just golden brown, about 30 minutes.

4. Add the salsify to the infused liquid and bring to a simmer over low heat. Cook until the salsify is just cooked through, about 15 minutes. Transfer to paper towels and pat dry. Discard the liquid. Using a Microplane grater over a large bowl, shave the hazelnuts to resemble thin wood shavings. Add the chestnut flour and toss with the parsley, fennel fronds, and tarragon. Set aside.

5. In a medium sauté pan, melt the butter over medium heat. Add the salsify and cook until the butter becomes a medium-dark brown and has a toasty aroma, 3 to 5 minutes. Stir in the remaining ½ tsp salt and 1 tsp honey, and remove from the heat.

6. One at a time, roll the salsify in the herb-nut mixture and crisscross a few salsify "logs" on each plate. Sprinkle the dill and chives over. Serve immediately.

SERVES 4 TO 6

SCALLOPS IN PARSLEY-ROOT MILK WITH FROZEN PEAR ICE

In this poetic composition from Matt Lightner's hide-and-seek cuisine, scallops hibernate under a dome of pear ice as a few boisterous dandelion leaves dance on top and earthy parsley-root milk pools nearby. It's everything you'd expect from a vision of spring emerging from winter: an edible white landscape with just an eye-catch of green and quietly intense flavors. The pear ice gets a complex bump from mead—a growing Oregon obsession—and the scallops gain a yeasty-sweet fragrance from kasu, the solid by-product of pressing sake, found at Japanese groceries. If you don't have a juicer, substitute 1 cup store-bought unsweetened pear juice and ½ cup water for the pears.

Pear Ice

5 firm unripe pears, peeled

½ cup/120 ml mead or hard cider

2½ tbsp apple cider vinegar

Parsley-Root Milk

3 fresh Hamburg parsley roots or parsnips, peeled

1 cup/240 ml whole milk

1½ tbsp sugar

½ tsp fine sea salt

2 tbsp kasu

¼ cup/60 ml olive oil

½ tsp fine sea salt

4 large diver scallops

4 fresh Hamburg parsley roots or parsnips, peeled

1 tsp high-quality olive oil

½ lemon

20 wild fresh dandelion leaves

1. TO MAKE THE PEAR ICE: Juice the pears in a juicer. Strain the juice into a small, deep tray or loaf pan, and stir in the mead and vinegar. Freeze until rock hard, a few hours or overnight.

2. TO MAKE THE PARSLEY-ROOT MILK: Coarsely chop the parsley roots. In a medium saucepan, combine the chopped parsley root, milk, sugar, and salt and cook over medium heat until very tender, about 15 minutes. Transfer to a food processor or blender and purée until smooth. Over a bowl, strain through a fine-mesh sieve. Cover and chill 1 hour, until cold.

3. In a medium bowl, whisk together the kasu, olive oil, and salt. Toss in the scallops and chill for 30 minutes. Finely grate the parsley roots into a medium bowl.

4. Meanwhile, heat a charcoal grill to medium.

5. Rinse the scallops and pat dry with paper towels. Grill until lightly charred and still rare in the middle, about 1 minute on each side. Cool the scallops briefly, and then tear them into ¼-in-/6-mm-wide threads.

6. Scatter the scallop threads randomly onto four plates and drizzle with a little of the high-quality olive oil and a squeeze of juice from the lemon. Spoon about 3 tbsp of the parsley-root milk over each serving, letting it drip over the scallops and onto the plates, and then sprinkle with 1 to 2 tbsp of the grated parsley root. Using a fork, scrape 2 to 3 tbsp of the pear ice into a fine powder over each serving of the scallops, and scatter the wild dandelion leaves over the top. Serve immediately.

SERVES 4

KEVIN GIBSON

EVOE

A perfectionist conquers the seasons with a grill pan and a make-do playbook.

Imagine you've wandered into a cooking show, but the audience is just you. Standing in what looks like a dorm room decorated by Sur La Table, a chef works silently at a butcher block that triples as prep station, dining counter, and one man's vision of "eat local," conjured with a grill pan and mysterious jars of pickled secrets. Scan the wall-size blackboard menu, every inch crammed with possibility, call out your order, and Kevin Gibson begins performing like a biology professor on *Restaurant: Impossible*. Welcome to Evoe.

Gibson is a chef's chef. Peers talk about him with a kind of reverence usually reserved for retiring baseball stars. While Portland's food scene catches fire with DIY cool and bratty animal cooking, Gibson, shy and introverted, shrugs and goes his own way, snooping out yanked-from-the-earth inspirations for plates of calm sophistication. He's the guy you always see at the farmers' market trying to find the perfect chickweed. It has never been his mission to change the face of cooking. Day after day, he just quietly does what everyone talks about: makes great food.

A few years ago, Gibson slipped away from his lofty kitchen, bidding goodbye to the pressure of delivering the Last Supper in a city where a $65 meal carries the expectations of a deathbed food wish. Now he shines comet-bright in his own universe, making enlightened snacks in the midst of Portland's hippie haven on Southeast Hawthorne. At Evoe, he's a one-man band; help comes from his boss and neighbor, Pastaworks, a boutique grocery store where he's free to forage the aisles like a contestant on *Supermarket Sweepstakes*. Regulars come just to see how he's responding to his latest rations: fresh oysters, sea beans (a kind of salty beachcomber's asparagus), or perhaps Oregon-coast glacier lettuce, an edible succulent with a permafrost glow and a wild chew, which Gibson pairs with juicy peaches and crisp, smoky speck.

Even by Portland standards, Evoe is quirky. Hours are noon to seven. You sit on stools and pay at Pastawork's cash register next door. But for anyone who loves to eat real food—personal and affordable, with peerless ingredients—it's Exhibit A in the case for why Portland is the envy of the country.

The Deviled Eggs Are in the Details

Food formulas don't exist at Evoe. Nor do heat lamps. Gibson assembles dishes to order, handing them to customers seated a lemon squirt away. The menu responds only to Gibson's mood ring. If the muse calls, he might whip up four pâtés, wild boar to pheasant, with condiments gleaned from crab apples or wild plums snuck in the door by local growers. People whisper about his deviled eggs, little treasures crowned with changing whims, from fried duck cracklings to spicy chorizo crumbles, though insiders pray for the warm ones, grilled upside down, fluffy yolk filling and all, then flipped over to reveal a comforting blanket of toasty brioche crumbs and a crazy snort of fresh horseradish. Gibson, slightly befuddled by their cult status, confesses he never made a deviled egg before coming to Evoe.

Seafood also commands attention, sometimes as a heap of charred squid arriving under warm peaks of blood orange aïoli like some great meringue pie from the deep blue sea. And each season brings its own reward: spring morels spilling out of textbook-French omelets, winter duck posing with barely cooked persimmons, so fresh they taste like custard. Grilled cheese gets respect, too, as Gibson dogs a plug-in grill to find just the right amount of ooze and crunch.

When Evoe opened in 2007 as a low-budget Pastaworks experiment, the site lacked even a stove. When one finally arrived, it had electric burners, killing the nuances of heat and gas flames. For a food control freak like Gibson, it was a punch in the gut. But desperation is the mother of reinvention. Evoe's hyperfresh approach is, in part, a logistical response to minimal equipment and time constraints.

"I'm not a raw foodist or headed in that direction," says Gibson, who is tall and lanky and rides a motorcycle to work. "I'm just adapting to limitations. It's forced me to be creative."

Kevin Gibson, Raw and Uncut

With a countertop mandoline, the guillo-
tine of hand slicers, Kevin Gibson hyp-
notically transforms homely zucchini
into a vegetable you've never met before:
tongue-shaped curls of glistening green,
tasting not just moist but voluptuous. In
a moment, he's turned Susan Boyle into
Kim Kardashian. The man just wrings the
maximum out of minimalism. To eat a
Gibson dish is to taste poetry, pure
and simple.

"Being around him is so good for you,"
says Elias Cairo, a former Gibson dis-
ciple who now rules Portland's slow
salami scene at Olympic Provisions.
"His attention to detail. He never cuts
a corner. I even like his eccentric
bitterness. He gets distraught when a
restaurant does something half-ass.
A tiny stem in a salsa verde ruins
his day. I love that about him."

Here are a few of Gibson's inside moves:

Porcini mushrooms: Gibson rethinks these
meaty mushrooms in a nearly naked forest
salad. Thinly slice the mushrooms,
sprinkle with fine sea salt, spritz with
enough Meyer lemon juice to dissolve the
salt, lightly massage just enough good
olive oil to coat, mound on a plate,
then hit with some crunchy fleur de sel
to finish. That's it. Sometimes he shaves
in fresh fennel. But the goal is to
preserve the porcini's "deep complex
bottom notes and a texture that just
snaps in your mouth."

Mâche: Gibson calls this wild lettuce
"the food-lover's watercress," and he
looks for the variety that grows into a
tight rosette. "The leaves add a walnut
note, a texture, that crunchy-fresh
thing. Lightly dressed mâche brings that
visual element to grilled scallops or a
cured meat plate. Looks pretty, tastes
great."

Artichokes: Let others steam and braise
away. Evoe has no time for such intense
labor! Gibson explores the little-known
beauty of the raw artichoke salad. Small
is best, as waste is less. Lop off
the top third, remove the spiky outer
leaves, trim away the outer stem, cut in
half, scoop out the fuzzy choke, and
then slice and dress with olive oil,
salt, lemon juice, finely chopped mint,
and thyme. "It's all edible, and you
get that wow factor."

EVOE'S SEASONAL SQUASH SALAD (TWO VARIATIONS)

The perfect Portland day involves taking off early from work and turning lunch into an afternoon at Evoe. Kevin Gibson keeps ingredients to a minimum, concentrating on high-quality everything in seasonal narratives made moments before serving. Food ideas are unlimited, he says. It's what you *don't* do that matters. These mandoline-sliced salads show how his basic building blocks ebb and flow with the weather, how summer fades to fall, green squash turns to gold, and soft cheese gives way to crunchy seeds.

SUMMER

Here, the squash is shaved but not peeled to show off the skins with a mix of handsome varieties like patty pan, Rome de Venise, and variegated zucchini. Ideally, use farm-fresh young squash, known for a solid, less seedy center. Or shave from the outside in, starting at the peel and stopping when you hit the core, where bitter notes hide. Keep things breezy with a good buttery olive oil, such as Arbequina or Taggiasca, adding just enough for a minimal shiny coat.

2 or 3 firm, young summer squash of different varieties, halved lengthwise

1½ tsp muscatel or sherry vinegar

1½ tbsp extra-virgin olive oil

Fleur de sel

¼ cup/40 g crumbled sheep's milk feta or ricotta salata, at room temperature

15 fresh mint leaves, torn into small pieces

Using a mandoline, cut the squash lengthwise into ⅛-in-/3-mm-thick slices, 4 to 5 in/10 to 12 cm long. Put the slices in a large bowl, drizzle with the muscatel and olive oil, and sprinkle with ½ tsp fleur de sel. Using your hands, toss gently to separate the slices and evenly coat. Heap an equal number of slices artfully onto each of four plates. Top with a scattering of cheese and mint, and finish with a healthy pinch of fleur de sel before serving.

SERVES 4

WINTER

Shaved fall squash reveals a meaty-sweet intensity, and, when finished with a swirl of aged balsamic, it borders on dessert. Peel and slice just before serving to preserve the fresh taste and succulent texture.

Heaping ¼ cup/55 g hulled raw pumpkin seeds

1 to 2 drops vegetable oil

Fleur de sel

1 small delicata, butternut, or acorn squash

1½ tsp balsamic vinegar aged 15 years

15 fresh mint leaves, torn into small pieces

1. In a small dry skillet, toast the pumpkin seeds over medium heat, shaking the pan occasionally to prevent scorching, until lightly browned, about 3 minutes. Transfer to a small bowl, immediately add the vegetable oil (just enough to barely moisten) and a pinch of fleur de sel, and toss to combine. Set aside.

2. With a vegetable peeler, peel the squash. Trim off the ends, and insert a spoon into the center to scrape out the seeds and stringy matter. Using a mandoline, slice the squash crosswise into paper-thin rounds. Put the squash in a large bowl, and continue until you have about 48 slices.

3. Drizzle the vinegar over the squash in a spiral pattern. Using your hands, toss gently, separating the slices to evenly coat. Heap about 12 slices artfully onto four plates. Top each serving with a scattering of pumpkin seeds and mint, and season with a healthy pinch of fleur de sel before serving.

SERVES 4

KEVIN'S CAULIFLOWER SOUP WITH FIVE VARIATIONS

Eat a Kevin Gibson soup and you'll swear you're inhaling pure cream; yet there's not a drop to be found. It helps to have super-fresh cauliflower and a feel for the vivid garnish. But Gibson swears it's all about the extreme purée, and he has burned through enough blenders to prove it. Purée in batches to add air and volume. "It adds something to the tongue," he says, "not quite pudding but very very light."

1¾ lb/800 g cauliflower, broken into florets, stem coarsely chopped

3 tbsp unsalted butter

1 medium onion, finely chopped

2 tsp Meyer lemon juice

2 tsp fine sea salt

1. In a stainless-steel pot, bring salted water to a boil over high heat. Blanch the cauliflower for a few minutes, or until just barely tender. Drain well, transfer to a large bowl, and set aside.

2. Using the same pot, melt the butter over medium heat. Add the onion and sauté until translucent, about 7 minutes. Stir in the cauliflower. Add enough cold water to barely cover and bring to a simmer over medium-high heat. Reduce the heat to low and cook until soft, about 20 minutes.

3. Purée the soup, one small batch at a time, in a blender (holding the lid down). Strain through a sieve back into the pot. Season with the lemon juice and salt. Stir over low heat until hot enough to serve. (If the soup seems too thick, thin with a little water.)

SERVES 4

Five Variations for Cauliflower Soup

Fried duck cracklings: Save ends of duck skin and fat in the freezer in a covered container. Thaw and render over very low heat until crisp and golden brown, about 20 minutes. Sprinkle the crispy nuggets over the top of the soup for bold crunch and rich depth.

Brioche croutons: For a buttery crunch, toast very small cubes of brioche, then pile a few in the center of each serving. Scatter finely chopped chives around the perimeter to finish.

Caviar and crème fraîche: Whip up some crème fraîche until nice and fluffy, then mix in a little caviar, lemon juice, and chives. Spoon a dollop into each bowl and top with more caviar.

Fresh crab and lemon: Spoon a little shredded Dungeness crabmeat on top of each serving, then add a good squeeze of lemon juice. Or make a salad of chives, crab, and Meyer lemon, and spoon on top of the soup.

Seared scallops and chives: Sear four large diver scallops and cut each one in half horizontally. Lean two halves against each other on top of each serving of soup. Garnish the scallops with fleur de sel and the soup with some finely chopped chives.

MARK DOXTADER
TASTEBUD

Local foods glow from a wood oven roaming the great outdoors.

Mark Doxtader had never laid a brick in 1998 when he got the idea to build a 3,500-pound wood-burning oven, haul it to the Portland Farmers' Market, and unleash his love of baking. To transport the beast, he gave it a permanent home in the back of his truck. On day one, he wasn't taking any chances. At five o'clock in the morning, his father drove behind him to the downtown site, packing extra bricks and mortar, just in case disaster struck. He pulled in without a hitch. Hours later, Doxtader lit a fire with freshly chopped wood, and when the coals burned brightly, he laid down a vision of flatbread topped with just-picked apples, a nod to his gig as an organic farmer. Market-goers swarmed like moths to flames. To Doxtader, it felt like home, community.

Things heated up quickly at his Tastebud booth, as Doxtader's wood-fired cobblers started a stampede. Sometimes he made eight varieties at once, showcasing his home-grown fruits in spreads that could embarrass the State Fair ladies. The jumbo squares boasted imposing walls of crust, whole-grain perfumes, and hot, juicy interiors. But mostly they tasted of urgency. Fresh? Doxtader's 1966 Ford pickup had been barreling down I-5, sparks flying from a raging 650°F oven locked and loaded with baking cobblers, minutes before the tasty treats hit customers' fingers,

The golden beauties were "cooked to perfection" during the thirty-minute ride to the market. The oven door caught fire on the highway on more than one occasion, Doxtader now confesses. But no worries, he says. "We just pulled over and took out the fire extinguishers."

As the cobblers' popularity took off, so did demand for Tastebud's pizza—fire-puffed slices holding whatever catches his eye from a neighboring farm booth. That might mean kale flowers, white pumpkin slices, or perhaps garlic whips, which he partners with roasted morels and pungent Italian cheese. Even among the legends who populate Portland's market scene—Roger, The Mushroom Man; and Gene Thiel, the godfather grower who talks to his carrots—Doxtader is iconic in his plaid shirt and towering presence. Nobody knows these heirloom-stocked aisles better. Doxtader has an instinct, an internal GPS that tracks the premier finds of the day. The sweetest corn, the most buttery pears inevitably climb into the jaws of Tastebud's furnace.

But by 2008, the ever-present throngs took a toll on the gentle giant. One Saturday, word spread that Doxtader was done with his cobbler and pizza show for the year, or maybe forever. Regulars wailed in despair. Doxtader, the Neil Young of market vendors, the keeper of the flame, the guardian of integrity, the embodiment of everything good and real about Portland's food culture, has that effect on people.

Number of miles on Tastebud's oven:
11,868

Bagels with a Point of View

Doxtader's passion for artisan bread and local flavors led to another brainstorm: Montreal-style bagels, boiled in honeyed water and wood-fired, according to Canadian scripture. The finished beauties could then be slathered with Tastebud's

brand of terroir: fat berries, roasted squash, wild salmon lox, pickled green tomatoes, and other essences of the moment. "I'm just a medium," he says with a shrug, "a showcase for the market."

In 2009, Tastebud Bagels was born at the weekly Hillsdale Farmers' Market in Southwest Portland, a stronghold for Portland's small Jewish community. Every Sunday morning, Doxtader arrived in the parking lot at six o'clock and, in near darkness, fired up a couple of cauldrons on a camping stove. He rolled his bagels on a giant cutting board, twelve at a time, boiled them for two minutes, and then popped the circles into his glowing oven in the back of his truck. By the time customers arrived at ten a.m., they found little miracles to rival anything in New York: small, compact rounds, each faintly sweet, a little smoky, and carpeted with a black seedy crunch. Word quickly leaked that Hillsdale was the hideout for Portland's best bagels—all 250 of them.

Suddenly, Doxtader found himself in a familiar situation. Lines formed before the market even opened. "I'll take a dozen, dude," bellowed one of the first customers. The words were not music to Doxtader's ears. Supplies were quickly ravished, and Doxtader had to reach deep to find his inner junta leader. Rationing orders went into effect. The new rule: only a few bagels per person.

"At one point the line was ten booths long," Doxtader recalls. "Some days we sold out in forty-five minutes. It was a spectacle." Let's just say that mild-mannered Portlanders, the people who never honk, are as polite as Cain and Abel when the last Tastebud bagels are in play.

Baby, It's Coals Outside

"Oh wow, man. Look at THAT! I need some of that," a man yelled excitedly, holstering his umbrella and locking down his eyes like a dog during a cheeseburger sighting.

On a recent wintery Saturday, *"that"* debuted at the Saturday farmers' market in downtown Portland: a thirty-five-pound hunk of porchetta as big as a wrestler's thigh, stuffed with fresh-made sausage, and pulled from Tastebud's furnace around eleven in the morning. Within minutes, a knife big enough to frighten Jack Bauer came out, and the sandwich making began. The adventure extended to oven-fresh focaccia bread and dueling red and green salsas—a couple of extra dabs of *oh yeah* to welcome juicy slices of local pork raised, like all good Oregonians, on a diet of hazelnuts.

After ten years on the farmers' market circuit, Doxtader has learned this: If he builds a fire, they will come. He's just more relaxed about it now. After all, he chose this nomadic vendor life. After bailing from photography school in Southern California, he chose to cook in the cold much of the year, standing in puddles, battling Portland's sideways rain and winds with only a canvas roof to protect culinary "display cases" repurposed from weathered doors. "Maybe I was recovering from L.A., but I wanted to do something righteous, with no questions about morality," he explains. "Cooking outdoors is a huge part of what keeps me going. I used to try to make elaborate meals over campfires. It was primitive but fun. I've tried to make that tangible in the city."

Doxtader sold his farm a few years back. His wood oven now stars at six farmers' markets a week, with a different menu for each location. The pizzas are back, and, on Saturdays, the oven spits out the original flatbread in salty flaps as big as a queen-size pillow. Meanwhile, Tastebud bagels are a fixture everywhere.

Four nights a week, Doxtader also runs Tastebud, the restaurant, a low-key Southeast Portland spot mostly frequented by food lovers and local chefs. His latest project is Wednesday Night Chicken Dinners, featuring smoky biscuits, rough-smashed potatoes, and roasted vegetables that taste straight from the ground. Hidden at the bottom of the menu: the return of Tastebud's famed berry cobblers, $6 each.

Don't tell anyone.

Mark Doxtader Lights His Fireplace

Mark Doxtader first practiced cooking using his fireplace hearth and campground pits. In his world, when the temperature rises, everything tastes better, even Peeps. High heat makes amazing things happen: a crackle of crust, a seductive moisture, a smoky perfume. Here are three ways he lights it up:

Whole corn in the fireplace—"Wait until the coals are extremely hot—glowing red—then pop the whole husks on top, rotating with long tongs until the husks are well charred. Remove and peel like a banana, halfway down, and slather with good butter, kosher salt, and fresh ground pepper."

Roasted Peeps—"I hate s'mores, but I love toasted marshmallows—how the sugar gets really brittle and caramel colored. Nothing beats a Peep, or, better yet, a *stale* Peep, which can withstand the fire even better."

Salmon collars—"Toss the collars in a little olive oil, lemon juice, salt, and pepper. When the wood burns down to hot coals, carefully set a grill over the glowing heat. Add the collars, and sear until nice and hot, about 2 minutes on each side, turning with long-handled tongs."

WHOLE LEMON AND RAW ASPARAGUS PESTO

Forget basil leaves and pine nuts. To push the concept of "pesto" into a vivid reckoning of spring, Mark Doxtader extracts the power of raw asparagus and whole lemons—pulp, skins, and all. The result: tart and grassy, and wildly delicious. Toss with pasta, spoon over fish, or, in classic Tastebud mode, dab on bagels bearing cream cheese and crispy bacon. For a cool garnish, roast a couple of the spears in a hot oven with a little olive oil and salt.

2 lb/910 g asparagus, tough ends trimmed

1 whole lemon, halved crosswise and seeded

4 garlic cloves

1 handful fresh Italian parsley leaves

2 tbsp extra-virgin olive oil

1 tsp kosher salt

Pinch of freshly ground pepper

In a food processor, combine all the ingredients, including the lemon pulp and skins, and pulse to coarsely chop. Use immediately or cover and refrigerate up to 24 hours.

MAKES ABOUT 2 CUPS/455 G

TASTEBUD'S ORIGINAL BERRY COBBLER

The cobbler that launched a thousand smiles. Mixed berries are classic, but feel free to embrace the Tastebud spirit and grab whatever fruit smells the sweetest: pitted cherries, quartered plums, sliced peaches, even crab apples, and don't hesitate to serve with a couple scoops of vanilla ice cream.

2 cups/255 g whole-wheat flour

1 tsp baking powder

¼ tsp baking soda

½ tsp kosher salt

1 cup/200 g firmly packed brown sugar

¾ cup/170 g unsalted butter, chilled and cut into chunks

About ¼ cup/60 ml half-and-half

4 cups/600 g assorted berries

2 tbsp turbinado sugar

1. Preheat the oven to 425°F/220°C/gas 7. Butter a 13-by-9-in/33-by-23-cm baking dish.

2. In a bowl, combine the flour, baking powder, baking soda, salt, and brown sugar.

3. Using a pastry blender or your fingers, work the butter into the dry ingredients until marble-size chunks form. Add most of the half-and-half and gently stir, being careful not to overmix. The dough should feel just moist but still crumbly and stiff. Add more half-and-half if needed.

4. Press the dough evenly onto the bottom of the baking dish. Add the berries in an even layer, and then sprinkle the turbinado sugar over the top. Bake until the fruit is bubbling and the crust is golden brown, 20 to 25 minutes. Serve hot, cold, or at room temperature.

SERVES 8

TASTEBUD'S COBBLER TURNED CRISP VARIATION

1 cup/125 g oat flour or unbleached white flour

1 cup/85 g rolled oats

1 cup/200 g packed brown sugar

Pinch of salt

6 tbsp/85 g unsalted butter, chilled and cut into chunks

4 cups/600 g assorted berries or other fruit

2 tbsp turbinado sugar

1. Preheat the oven to 425°F/220°C/gas 7. Butter a 13-by-9-in/33-by-23-cm baking dish.

2. In a large bowl, combine the flour, oats, brown sugar and salt. Using a pastry blender or your fingers, work the butter into the dry ingredients until small pieces form and the mixture is somewhat combined. Chill for 20 minutes.

3. Sprinkle the berries into the baking dish and stir in the sugar. Distribute the topping evenly over the fruit, crumbling it with your fingers to break up the larger chunks.

4. Bake until the fruit is bubbling and the crisp topping is golden brown, 35 to 40 minutes. Serve warm.

fry chicken skin $1

Today

Limited

Than

NONG'S HOT SAUCE

NONG'S KHAO MAN GAI SAUCE

NONG'S THAI PALM SYRUP

FOR SALE!!
$4.99/each

CHAPTER 3

THE ASIAN STREET FOOD GANG

From ramen shops to animated whiskey lounges, Portland rethinks hawker cuisine for a new generation.

RAMEN

ANDY RICKER

POK POK +
PING +
WHISKEY SODA
LOUNGE

One Thai take-out food shack changes everything. Welcome to Rickerville, population: 1.

Andy Ricker didn't set out to create a foodie's paradise. He was simply on a mad quest to make the food he loves, to help us to understand what keeps driving him back to the Asian food street. He wanted to transport us to his haunts in Chang Mai and Bangkok—the night stalls, side woks, whiskey shacks, and riverboats that harbor a world of crazy eating, the best you can imagine, but rarely found in America.

Like Martin Scorcese breathing the streets of Little Italy, Ricker eats and lives Thai food culture. It gripped him twenty years ago, and he's been trekking to find it ever since, distilling its soul, finding its soundtrack. You'd have to look hard in America to find what this guy holds in his head. These aren't simple formulas readily found in cookbooks; they rely on one man's determination to wander, discover, deconstruct, hunt down ingredients, and test, test, test to find the peak of perfection, the moment that fissions on the tongue. Ricker's cooking detonates on impact, marching into your mouth with canopies of herbs and heat bombs. Once you've tasted it, something happens. It's infectious and contagious, and there's no cure, no going back to what you've been eating for a lifetime: dumbed-down Thai menus apparently born in a secret cloning machine.

In 2005, Ricker—a sometimes surf bum, bass musician, bartender, and DJ—was painting houses to support his travels. But secretly, he was sketching the blueprint for his Thai food dream, Pok Pok. To Ricker, real estate's favorite motto—location, location, location—did not apply. Nail by nail, he hammered his vision in the driveway of a dilapidated Victorian home on car-zooming Division Street, where only the brave cross the road before reading their horoscope. Ricker's leap into the void would eventually lead to massive credit card debt, a mortgaged home, no operating funds, and sleepless nights pushing the boundaries of his sanity. His game plan looked roughly like this:

Phase One: Build a tiny take-out shack next to a decrepit Southeast Portland house. Name: Pok Pok. Nickname: "The Shack." Create the feel of late-night noshing in Bangkok with the eating hut and Asian pop music. Add outdoor cooks wielding giant pestles that create the thwacking sound of Thai food: *pok, pok, pok, pok.* Charcoal-grill whole birds outside, just like in Bangkok, and serve *khao soi kai* (curry noodle soup) as the gods meant it to be: with chile paste hot enough to part your hair on the opposite side.

Phase Two: While the shack hums along, work fifteen hours a day converting the home's daylight basement into an Asian food lounge that looks like a junior-high make-out party room circa 1965. Fill it with rec-room veneer, teeny tables, chubby booths with the sheen of black licorice, a rough-hewn bar, and a no-reservations policy. Add beer, whiskey flights, and fizzy things called "drinking vinegars."

In Ricker's dreamscape, Western compromises were out of the question, even if it meant losing his rock 'n' roll T-shirt. Pok Pok would have no trite honky formulas, no stir-fried this and pick-your-protein that, no "Do you want that mild, medium, or hot?" In fact, Pok Pok would have no English translations. Diners can learn how to pronounce the names! Above all, there would be no chopsticks, except for with noodles; in Thailand, spoons are the mode of cutlery.

Moreover, Ricker refused to serve America's favorite Thai noodle dish, *pad Thai*, (or *phat Thai* to the authentic crowd); never mind his reputation among friends for making the best ever. Ricker feared this would spell The End, an exit strategy for diners looking for the familiar. Put *phat Thai* on the menu, and no one will order anything else.

Friends wondered: Did the guy have a death wish?

"Remember that scene in *Drugstore Cowboy*, when Matt Dillon is living in that horrible hotel at the end? That's what it felt like when we saw this property," says Adam Levey, an accomplished photographer and Ricker's best friend. "He committed to this space without asking anyone's advice, put his ass and his money on the line, then invited four of us to see it. He was talking about having a chicken shack, and building a restaurant in this awful basement, in a white neighborhood with no safety nets. He was just so excited about making actual Thai food, what he truly loved. It was terrifying to anyone watching the process. We were just hoping he didn't end up killing himself."

No one was prepared for what happened: six dishes, three outdoor tables, and one little shack blew away Portland's food scene. Endless lines at the Pok Pok shack left no doubt; Portlanders were willing to endure punishment, huddling in a handmade hut on rain-soaked nights to taste the genuine. From the takeout window came a whole new experience. Heady noodles and sweet pork wonders sent taste buds flying, and a quiet, driven guy in a knit cap flashed a prophetic glimpse of Portland's food-cart scene.

Ricker reserves a fuller expression of Thai cuisine for his clandestine basement eatery. Followers jam in for plates of *yam samum phrai*, an herbal nut salad shrouded with sawtooth, betel, basil, and lime leaves, all cut as thin as needles. This is Ricker in one complex bite: grassy, soapy, spicy, crunchy, complex, and supremely refreshing; you can't inhale it fast enough. Some come for lunch and then return for dinner, eating as if in a fever dream, hunched over plates of crispy, caramelized, fire-breathing, garlic speckled, fish-sauce–singing chicken wings with an enthusiasm that calls up your worst images of cannibalism.

Portland's food bloggers liken Pok Pok's food to crack-cocaine, especially the dish officially titled on the menu as Ike's Fish Sauce Chicken Wings. "Thai food is addictive," says Ricker. "*I'm* addicted to it. I have to have a dish, and, suddenly, I'm on a plane again."

> Weight of birds needed to feed the demand for Pok Pok's chicken wings: **2,700 pounds a week**
>
> Admits Ricker: "They pay the mortgage."

Triumph of the Grill

The thing you have to realize about Andy Ricker is that he's working it, day and night. No one asked him to improve on Pok Pok's signatures, the eight or ten dishes whose removal from the menu would be received as mortal wounds by his fans. But here he is, adding limestone paste to the cooking water for his sticky rice to better approximate Thailand's harder water. On some days you'll find him checking the aroma levels of *yam wun sen*, a dish of zinged-out glass noodles made with Chinese celery, homemade sour pork sausage, pickled garlic whacked right off the heads, and garlic oil for good measure. It makes your entire body buzz. According to Ricker, Thai people place as much weight on smell as taste. "If you can't smell the celery, it's not right."

But only fools stick to Pok Pok's mainstays, as new taste fixations appear every time he journeys back to his

power source. After a recent sojourn, Portlanders were suddenly forking into southern Thai noodles tangled with grilled pineapple, pungent dried shrimp, a few of those nuclear Thai chiles, and a wash of sweet coconut cream, thick and creamy. Yin meets yang; heaven crashes into fiery earth, and to hog it for yourself is not only authentic, it's encouraged.

Still, there's no "right" way to make this food. Twenty Chang Mai vendors might serve the same dish, yet no two are alike. Ricker's MO is to check them all out, often multiple times, notebook in hand, filling entire pages with observations like a forensic detective working the evidence locker. Preferred versions are re-created in his kitchen lab, but artistic impulses are banished, leaving only true ingredients and the natural-born gift that Ricker would deny: his ability to make anything taste better, even tradition.

As Pok Pok's repertoire has grown, so has its magical indoor/outdoor world. The funky yard scene has morphed into an exotic camp-out with Cambodian rock, heat lamps, twinkling Christmas lights, and the smell of sweet smoke wafting from grills that resemble old iron lungs. It's a remarkable vision of elsewhere, reimaged here, in the midst of a neighborhood pulsing with artisanal food carts,

blue-collar homes, and a rock 'n' roll ramen joint. Nothing quite like it exists anywhere.

Ricker is no longer a local secret. *Food & Wine* magazine calls Pok Pok "a shrine to Thai grilling." In 2011, Ricker won the James Beard Foundation Award for Best Chef Northwest, startling some of the white-jacketed old guard. Without question, he is now the country's foremost authority on Asian drinking foods. His other restaurants, Ping and the Whiskey Soda Lounge, are critical hits. Even New York greeted him like a conquering hero in 2012, as Pok Pok Wing marched into the Lower East Side with the country's best chicken wings and a media frenzy. Days before opening, the shop was blessed by chanting Thai monks, but Ricker seems to have all he needs. Bloggers record his every move, Pok Pok NY is drawing block-long waits, and the Pok Pok cookbook is in the works.

Ricker didn't plan to build an empire. "I just wanted to show that Thai food is so much more than what we usually see on menus," he says. "The depth and breadth of it gets to me; how much there is to discover."

To best friend Levey, it was a gutsy stand. "He saw this amazing gastronomy and believed in it. He studied this food and uplifted it in an egoless way. Eating those wings, your mouth smacking with all that sweet stuff and hot stuff, feels like your soul is getting a bubble bath."

Ricker didn't pander in order to survive, and it paid off, for him and for us.

"I get tears in my eyes thinking about how it turned out," says Levey. "He transformed Desolation Row into a place that changed everything."

Ping: A Steamy Revision of Chinatown

Ping opened in 2009 as a new kind of gathering spot, built on bold thinking in Chinatown's historic Hung Far Low Building. Ricker caught the attention of John Jay, the Asian youth culture oracle and branding guru of Wieden+Kennedy, a Portland advertising agency that counts Nike and Old Spice among its clients. Like Ricker, Jay is a cultural archaeologist, and according to *Fast Company* magazine, he's one of 2011's most influential business creatives. With partners Janet Jay and Kurt Huffman, Ricker and Jay transformed a forgotten corner in a tawdry neighborhood into a destination that looks nothing like Roman Polanski's *Chinatown*.

Under a light sculpture that evokes the mystery of the kimono sash with hanging folds of white paper and blood-red ribbons, customers inhale pork bone tea or deep-fried pork knuckles as big as your forearm. But the real find is *ju pa bao*, a kind of sublime pork chop slider, bone and all—just the thing to eat if you're hanging out in Macau, China, or . . . Portland, Oregon. Welcome to the new Mein Streets: daring, challenging, intriguing.

GQ's outspoken food critic Alan Richman ranked Ping number 4 on his 10 Best New Restaurants list in 2010, calling Ricker's steamed pork buns "a challenge to David Chang's preeminent version." But Ping's nonlinear list of skewers and Asian snacks has not been an easy sell. Ricker could have put Pok Pok's chicken wings on the menu and drawn lines down the block. But he was adamant: Ike's Wings were out of the question, off the table. Ping has its own mood, its own mission.

"Ping is not a place where everyone understands the dining experience from A to Z," says Ricker. "There's no 'Here's your salad, here's your entree.' It's a drinking and talking and eating place, like all over Southeast Asia. The focus is not to ooh and aah over every dish but to have fun with friends."

This is Ricker's lesson. Let the experience unfold. Don't overthink it. As he puts it, "Just grab it, and eat the damn thing." The joy is in the journey.

Whiskey Soda Lounge: The Return of *Phat Thai*

By late 2009, with Pok Pok looking like spring break in Fort Lauderdale, Ricker built the Whiskey Soda Lounge across the street as a holding pen for the hungry hordes. But it blossomed into something else: a psychedelic Asian-pop surf shack glowing like a jellyfish with shooting-star lights, spinning Shivas, and old Thai movies. This is the portal to Ricker's brain and his love letter to *aahaan kap klaem*, Thai pub snacks or "drinking foods." But at ten p.m., WSL shape-shifts into Ricker's *phat Thai* joint, at last, with six variations on the stir-fried noodle classic. The straight-up version packs the surprise of preserved radishes, dried tofu, and serious, nose-dripping heat. But *phat thai buu haw khai*, mingled with crab, then bound in a thin omelet, is a revelation, begging the question: "Where have the real versions been hiding?"

By Ricker's estimation, "Ninety-nine percent of the people in America don't care if you do the extra steps. It's just simple economics. Other Thai restaurants can make it in half the time, at half the cost, with ketchup and bean sprouts and chicken—and people love it. Thai cooking is very labor intensive for such a simple cuisine. What we're doing here is incredibly difficult, just tracking down all the ingredients."

To Ricker, that means dry-roasting imported Thai chiles over charcoal to obtain an unforgettable smoky heat, and, of course, finding the right spice grinder. It means nailing the ratios and the right cooking oil, rendered pork fat, a recent eureka following the ingestion of yet ten more versions during a two-week blitz through Thailand and China.

"There's an entire world in here," says Ricker, digging into his noodles one night. "But it's a pain in the ass."

Parting Thoughts

Three days after winning the James Beard award, Ricker was back to business, clamping down on Pok Pok's recipes, logging precise details for his staff as he readied for another month-long Thailand journey. "Nothing has really changed," he sighed. "I'm still showing cooks how to use goddamn charcoal."

The guy who stops at nothing to get it right recognizes the great irony of his existence: His most popular dish takes the least amount of thought: "It's insane how many chicken wings we sell but we have the formula down to a science. The wings are not what keep me up at night."

That honor goes to a new Pok Pok addition, *yam kai meuang*, a delicately aromatic northern Thai chicken soup made with free-running Asian roosters, prized for their lean, flavorful meat and superlative skin. Ricker recently found a source in California at a whopping cost of $20 a bird. "What do I worry about? Is the flavor correct? Is it too salty? Is the chicken cooked the right amount of time? There's so much knowledge that goes into this dish. We stew it, shred it, mix in Northern Thai curry paste, shrimp paste, spices, banana blossoms."

Despite all the work, *yam kai meuang* has few takers. Orders sold per night? One. Maybe three. Ricker's not dissuaded. With his telltale stoic determination, etched in a full frontal stare and blue eyes as clear as sea glass, he's making his stand: "It's utterly rustic. It's from another planet. I'm honestly excited about it. It stays."

POK POK'S GRILLED CORN WITH SALTY COCONUT CREAM AND LIMES

An occasional summer special at Pok Pok, Ricker's grilled corn was seemingly born in the backyard barbecue pit of paradise. If there's better corn on the cob anywhere, we haven't tasted it. The kitchen uses 100 percent UHT (ultra-high-temperature) coconut cream, sold in cans or jumbo juicelike boxes at Asian markets (favorite brand: Aroy-D), where you'll also find fresh or frozen green pandanus leaves, favored for their offbeat floral perfume.

1 pandanus leaf

2 cups/480 ml UHT coconut cream

1½ tbsp sugar

Kosher salt

12 ears shucked corn, stems intact

1 lime, cut into wedges for serving

1. Crumple the pandanus leaf into a medium saucepan. Stir in the coconut cream, sugar, and 1½ tsp salt. Bring to a boil over high heat, and then reduce the heat to low. Cover and simmer until reduced slightly, about 10 minutes. Set aside. (The cream can be refrigerated for up to 1 week.)

2. Heat a charcoal grill to medium-hot.

3. In a large pot, bring heavily salted water to a boil over high heat. Meanwhile, prepare a large bowl of ice water. Blanch the corn ears for 3½ minutes and immediately transfer with tongs to the ice bath to cool a few minutes. (You may need to cook the corn in batches.)

4. Place the ears on a baking sheet or large platter, and generously brush the reserved coconut cream over each ear. Place the ears on the grill, and grill until golden brown, 2 to 3 minutes per side. Transfer to a serving platter, and then brush with more cream and sprinkle with a little salt. Serve immediately with the lime wedges.

MAKES 12 EARS

PING'S GRILLED PORK COLLAR WITH SPICY ISAAN DIPPING SAUCE

This street classic is ubiquitous in Thailand, from beaches to back alleys, wherever a grill calls home. But count on Thai food archeologist Andy Ricker to find the best version: meat marinated in *shao hsing* (rice wine), ginger juice, and earthy cilantro root, then air-dried and finally dunked in northern Thai dipping sauce for another layer of tingling flavor. Ask your butcher for a pork collar, loved for its tenderness and rich cache of fat. The assemblage is simple, requiring only a field trip to an Asian grocery store and an overnight head start to marinate and dry the meat.

Pork Collar

One 6-oz/170-g chunk fresh ginger, juiced or grated and squeezed to make 3 tbsp juice

1 tbsp kosher salt

¹⁄₂ cup/120 ml honey

¹⁄₂ cup/120 ml *shao hsing* wine (rice wine) or whiskey

¹⁄₂ cup/120 ml Thai thin soy sauce

¹⁄₄ cup/60 ml sesame oil

1 oz/30g fresh cilantro root, coarsely pounded, or ¹⁄₄ cup/10 g chopped fresh cilantro stems

2 tbsp white peppercorns, coarsely pounded

One 4-lb/1.8-kg pork collar, shoulder, or loin, cut into 8 to 10 steaks

Isaan Dipping Sauce

1 tbsp Thai fish sauce (*nam pla*)

1 tbsp Thai thin soy sauce

1 tbsp sugar

2 tbsp water

1 tsp Golden Mountain or Maggi Seasoning Sauce

¹⁄₄ cup/60 ml fresh lime juice

¹⁄₄ cup/55 g dried, crushed Thai chiles

1 to 2 lemongrass stalks, finely chopped

1 tbsp finely chopped cilantro

1. TO PREPARE THE PORK COLLAR: In a large bowl, combine the ginger juice, salt, honey, wine, soy sauce, sesame oil, cilantro root, and peppercorns. Toss the pork into the marinade. Cover and refrigerate for 4 to 8 hours, turning once or twice.

2. Set a rack over a baking sheet. Using tongs, place the pork on the rack. Discard the marinade. Place the baking sheet in the refrigerator, uncovered, to air-dry the meat for about 4 hours. Remove from the refrigerator 1 hour before grilling to bring the meat to room temperature.

3. TO MAKE THE DIPPING SAUCE: In a large bowl, whisk together the fish sauce, soy sauce, sugar, water, seasoning sauce, lime juice, chiles, lemongrass, and cilantro. Set aside.

4. Heat a charcoal grill to medium-hot. Place the pork on the grill and cook until medium, 4 to 6 minutes on all sides. (If the flames start to flare up, remove the meat from the grill for a minute to let the fire subside, and then return it to the grill.) Transfer the cooked meat to a cutting board and let rest a few minutes. Cut the meat into bite-size pieces and arrange on a platter. Serve with the dipping sauce and cocktail forks or toothpicks.

SERVES 8 TO 10

WHISKEY SODA LOUNGE'S SKEWERED CHICKEN BUTTS

In Thailand, skewered chicken butts are known for their soft fat and toothsome, char-scented chew, perfectly captured at Andy Ricker's divey-cool bar. Seek them out at an Asian market. If you come up short, substitute boneless thighs.

¼ lb/115 g chicken butts or boneless chicken thighs

1 tbsp Thai fish sauce (*nam pla*)

½ tsp dried, crushed Thai chiles

Spicy Isaan Dipping Sauce (facing page)

1. Heat a charcoal grill to medium-hot.

2. In a large bowl, combine the chicken butts, fish sauce, and chiles. Marinate at room temperature for 10 minutes.

3. Meanwhile, soak six wooden skewers in water for 10 minutes to prevent them from burning on the grill.

4. Thread four chicken butts on each skewer. (Don't over-crowd or they won't crisp.) Grill the meat, without moving it, until crisp and slightly charred on one side, 3 to 4 minutes. Turn and cook the other side for a few minutes. Serve with the dipping sauce.

SERVES 4 TO 6

KOPITIAM TOAST WITH KAYA (COCONUT JAM)

One of the highlights of Ping is thick burnished toast and custardy coconut jam scented with thin, green, mile-long pandanus leaves, the vanilla of Southeast Asia. Andy Ricker picked up the habit at Malaysian Chinese coffee shops or *kopitiams*, where the bread is charcoal-fired and dispatched for breakfast with a side of animated conversation and local gossip. At Ping, people eat it between spicy dishes, like a celestial palate cleanser. Look for pandanus leaf, UHT (ultra-high-temperature) coconut cream, and Japanese pan bread at Asian markets.

1 pandanus leaf

1 cup/240 ml UHT coconut cream

3 eggs

2 egg yolks

¾ cup/150 g extra-fine sugar

¼ tsp kosher salt

1 small loaf thickly sliced Japanese pan bread or Texas toast

1. In a small saucepan, bring the pandanus leaf and coconut cream to a low boil over medium heat. Immediately reduce the heat to low and simmer for 10 minutes. Remove from the heat and cool to lukewarm. Remove the leaf and discard.

2. In a medium bowl, whisk the eggs, egg yolks, sugar, and salt. Slowly drizzle in the coconut cream, whisking constantly to combine. Strain the mixture into the top of a double boiler (or into a stainless-steel bowl set over a pan of simmering water) and cook over medium-low heat, stirring often, until thick, glossy, and smooth, about 30 minutes.

3. Lightly toast eight slices of the bread and cut each one in half on the diagonal. Spread 1 tbsp or so of the jam over each triangle and serve immediately. Store leftover jam in a covered glass jar in the refrigerator for up to 2 months.

SERVES 8

TAMARIND WHISKEY SOUR

Not lollipop sweet, not weirdly bitter, and, heavens no, not mixology. An Andy Ricker drink is a rarity, one built on surprise yet very food-friendly. This one is a signature of his Asian street-food empire, rocketing around your mouth with an extra pop of amerena cherries (Italian sour cherries resting in sweet syrup). Asian markets are a good source for tamarind pulp and palm sugar, often sold in solid small discs.

¼ cup/70 g wet seedless tamarind

2¾ cups/660 ml boiling water

8 oz/225 g palm sugar

1¼ cups/300 ml bourbon, preferably Early Times

¾ cup/180 ml freshly squeezed lime juice

8 large scoops of ice cubes

½ orange, cut crosswise into thin half-moons

8 amerena cherries, skewered on toothpicks

1. Place the tamarind in a medium heat-proof bowl and cover with 1¾ cups/420 ml of the boiling water. Let cool for 30 minutes. Using a potato masher or fork, mash the pulp to incorporate it with the water, and then pass the mixture through a food mill or coarse sieve.

2. Put the palm sugar in a small heat-proof bowl and cover with the remaining 1 cup/240 ml boiling water. Whisk until the sugar is dissolved. Chill the syrup for 15 minutes.

3. In a pitcher, stir together the tamarind, palm syrup, bourbon, and lime juice.

4. Add a scoop of ice to a cocktail shaker, add about ¾ cup/240 ml of the tamarind mixture, and shake well until chilled. Pour into a double rocks glass. Garnish with an orange slice and a cherry. Repeat to make the remaining drinks.

MAKES 8 COCKTAILS

PATRICK FLEMING
BOKE BOWL

A pop-up restaurant revamps the ramen shop with joyful hedonism.

They are Portland's unlikely food revolutionaries: a country-club chef, a commercial pilot, and an events promoter liberating bowls of ramen. In short: three white guys in their forties, armed with Facebook alerts and fresh ideas about Japan's famously addictive soup. The trio draws mini flash mobs to dining adventures far removed from the traditional noodle shop, let alone that dorm-room classic, the supermarket instant ramen packet. Boke Bowl, their monthly experiment in food and social media, is the place to be: an itinerant, pop-up ramen rave shaped by compulsive cooking, word of mouth, and blog buzz.

Behind the makeshift stove is Patrick Fleming, who tackles home food projects like a dog with a sock, fiercely and unrelentingly while juggling shifts as executive chef at the Oregon Golf Club in suburban West Linn. To commune with the gods of smoked meat, Fleming spent four years brining, dry-rubbing, and perfuming enough haunches to frighten an Eastern Oregon cattle rancher. During a year-long quest to master the great Asian dumpling, he crimped hundreds in a day. His passion for meat craft and homemade noodles led to a ramen immersion and then a brainstorm: to serve playful versions in changing locations posted on the Internet. To Fleming, creativity and lively social exchange trump textbook authenticity. He imagined pork-a-holics, hard-core vegans, and gluten-phobes at the same table with artistic noodles, broths, and toppings for all—glimpsing the future of finicky dining. If things went well, he'd have a ready-made audience for a future restaurant. It could be like *American Idol* . . . without the bad singing.

Two college friends jumped on board: pilot Brannon Riceci as business partner/front man and food-connected Tim Parsons as consigliere. In the first move, Parsons posted a sneak peek of Fleming's eye-popping ramen on his Facebook page, quickly eliciting upturned thumbs and cries from the curious: "What's *that*? I want it now!" Boke Bowl was born.

Month one, September 2010: Two hundred eaters waited in the rain at a tiny bar in Southeast Portland as Fleming boiled six vats of ramen in a tented sidewalk kitchen worthy of a MASH unit while a DJ spun old 45s. In the powerful, teenage-crush language of Facebook, exclamation points abounded ("oh.my.god. YUM!!"). Six months later: Boke Bowl's website draws 20,000 page views a month, and Boke happenings, staged at different restaurants on

off-nights, are packed. In one swoop, Fleming and company tapped Portland's triple love of WiFi, the ecstatically hand-made, and, yes, the endless waits in line for good food.

Their success is generated in part by the dramatically changing backdrops, swanky to funky, derived from the willingness of rent-paying restaurants to let freewheeling experimenters occupy their house for a night and a small fee. "It's much easier to try something here, without the pressure, without the bling," says Fleming, who has a strong head of sandy hair and a soft, boyish smile. "Egos don't rule in Portland. Few chefs in other cities would allow you to take over their space."

Boke by the Numbers

Hours required to make 200 orders of ramen noodles: **8**

Number of days to make a proper ramen stock: **3**

Most expensive investment: **$1,600 pasta machine**

Noodle Freaks and Geeks

That slurping sound you hear in New York, Los Angeles, and Vancouver, B.C.—cities where "rameniacs" scour the streets like Will Smith seeking a postapocalyptic virus cure—is only a muted sip in Portland, making Boke a local hero. In Japan, where the noodle fanatics make the soccer nuts look pale and withdrawn, dozens of variations and regional versions thrive in an estimated 80,000 outposts. Still, standards are understood. For ramenistas, it's about the depth of the broth and how it balances with the springy noodles and the *tare*, or finishing sauce, the thing that brings it home, what disciples call the soul of ramen.

Fleming has studied the form, taken the elements apart, and rebuilt them as a kind of one-man carnival jug-gling handmade noodles, intricate stocks demanding days of spicing and roasting, and complex proteins transformed by herbaceous oils and clouds of smoke. Boke's break from the pack is clear in a black cod ramen born out of fish bone juices, toasted sardines, and two kinds of miso, all fortified by a *tare* of shrimp shells, shallots, and sake. Even the vegan ramen, bobbing beneath just-made butternut squash rice cakes, gets the full three-ring treatment.

Ramen, with Heart and Fried Chicken

Boke's universe extends to jaw-shaped buns clamped around soft charred eggplant, six kinds of Japanese pickles, and, for a closing argument, miso butterscotch Twinkies. Plenty of inspiration comes from David Chang's *Momofuku* cookbook, as Fleming likes the way New York's bad-boy superstar applies Western techniques, artfully and confidently, to Asian street food. But Fleming's ability to feed possessed hordes with military precision draws from his far-flung experiences as a New Orleans high-schooler, Seattle grunge-rock festival caterer, London "kitchen bitch" at the Michelin-starred Lettonie in Bath (where even ice cream scooping was an earned stripe), and, currently, Portland dad and recovering drug addict.

Fleming's fix is now food. He concocts everything feasible down to his own spin on the fiery Sriracha hot sauce typically found in plastic bottles, a nuanced condiment he calls "Hot Boke." The guy can wring surprise from lumps of Brussels sprouts, crisping the leaves, caramelizing the cores, adding blood oranges, and, for good measure, tossing in tofu as you've never seen it: cubed, brined, smoked, and deep-fried into crazy croutons breathing fish sauce, lime, and chile pickles.

But nothing quite matches the happy hedonism of ramen teeming with pulled pork and topped by teetering pieces of heaven: double-floured, super-crispy, buttermilk fried chicken dripping with aïoli, itself a miracle of may-onnaise, cucumber crunch, and pickled mustard seeds swollen like fat orange dots. This is the Boke's moment of glory: Tokyo comfort, Southern soul, and Portland passion in one bold slurp.

Why push himself to the brink? "I've had to push myself in so many directions to keep myself motivated," says Fleming. "All my passions just culminated in ramen. It's twenty years in a bowl."

Epilogue

Fourteen months after launching the quintessential Portland food experience, Boke Bowl opened as a brick-and-mortar in the rising culinary no man's land of the industrial Southeast. Fleming now stands in a gleaming alley of stainless steel, backed by investors and diners furiously knocking back noodle soups at handsome communal tables. This is the best of Portland's food scene: a design-savvy, unpretentious, affordable celebration of the art of eating. Exclaimed one jubilant eighty-nine-year-old diner: "It's like Thanksgiving at a homeless table. I love it."

The Zen of Boke

On trust, tofu, and David Chang:
"No one really likes tofu. I've had soil that tasted better. It's been my obsession to make it taste better. I found some fresh tofu in Portland and decided to treat it like meat: smoke it, brine it, deep-fry it. This is what resonated most about D. Chang's book: Trust your skill set and apply it."

On the enlightenment of sweet, sour, smoky, salty, and spicy: "There's a reason Americans eat vats of barbecue sauce. I try to get all of these elements in every bowl, salad, and pickle."

On heavenly miso: "My secret ingredient, an instant hit of smoky, salty, and sweet. When I need depth, I go to light miso. I even fold it into butter to finish off mushrooms."

On the art of brining: "Essential for lean meats like pork, turkey, and chicken. Brining breaks down the proteins and allows the salt to penetrate deeply. Pass on this step and you can season away, but you won't get there."

On practicing caramelization: "I caramelize everything—apples, onions, fennel. Half of the vegetables in our vegan ramen are caramelized really low and slow to bring out the natural sweetness. The importance of caramelized flavors was hammered home by San Francisco chef Julia McClasky, who called me out more than once, 'You call that seasoning?'"

HOT BOKE SAUCE

Always on Boke's table: homemade Sriracha sauce, with all of the heat of the addictively spicy Thai "ketchup" to match a new layer of smoky resonance. Spice wimps can go mellow by using fewer chile pepper seeds.

2 lb/910 g red jalapeños, halved lengthwise

¼ cup/60 ml olive oil

20 garlic cloves, coarsely chopped

4 medium shallots, coarsely chopped

1 tbsp kosher salt

5 tbsp/60 g sugar

½ cup/120 ml unseasoned rice vinegar

2 tbsp sherry vinegar

½ cup/60 g tomato paste

1 tbsp soy sauce

1 tbsp Korean chile powder or paprika

½ cup/120 ml water

1. Remove the seeds from half of the jalapeños (or, if you like it spicier, leave all of the seeds). In a large stainless-steel pot, warm the olive oil over medium heat. Add the jalapeños, garlic, shallots, and salt. Cook over medium-low heat until the jalapeños soften and the juices are released, about 20 minutes.

2. Stir the sugar, rice vinegar, sherry vinegar, tomato paste, soy sauce, chile powder, and water into the pot and bring to a low simmer. Cook, stirring occasionally, until reduced and thick, about 1 hour.

3. Transfer the sauce to a blender and purée on high (holding down the lid) until smooth. Strain through a sieve into a bowl to remove the seeds. Store in a covered glass jar for up to 1 month in the refrigerator.

MAKES 1 QT/960 ML

MISO-BUTTERSCOTCH TWINKIES

These are not your father's Twinkies. Boke Bowl's delicate beauties come with obsessive touches like vanilla beans scraped into the batter, thanks to pastry gal Elizabeth Green. Miso paste, of all things, lends a *dulce de leche* flavor profile to the filling. Secure a nonstick éclair pan in advance, available online and at kitchen shops. Save leftover pudding for a bonus dessert, best topped with whipped cream.

Twinkies

Vegetable oil, for greasing the pan

¾ cup/90 g unbleached all-purpose flour

1½ tsp baking powder

½ tsp kosher salt

5 eggs, separated

1 cup/200 g granulated sugar

1 vanilla bean, split lengthwise

¼ tsp pure vanilla extract

2 tbsp sour cream

Miso-Butterscotch Pudding

3 eggs

1 tbsp pure vanilla extract

¼ cup plus 2 tbsp/45 g cornstarch

1½ cups/360 ml heavy cream

1 cup/200 g granulated sugar

2 tbsp light corn syrup

¼ cup/60 ml water

½ tsp lemon juice

2 tbsp molasses

6 tbsp/85 g unsalted butter

3 tbsp light miso paste

1 cup/240 ml whole milk

Powdered sugar for topping

1. TO MAKE THE TWINKIES: Generously coat a nonstick 8-cup éclair pan with the vegetable oil. Preheat the oven to 350°F/180°C/gas 4.

2. Sift the flour, baking powder, and salt into a small bowl. Set aside.

3. Using a stand mixer fitted with the whisk attachment, beat the egg yolks and ½ cup/100 g of the sugar on medium-high until pale yellow and doubled in volume, 4 to 5 minutes. Using the dull side of a knife, scrape the vanilla bean seeds from the pod into the mixture. (Reserve the pod for another use.) Reduce the speed to low, add the vanilla extract and sour cream, and mix until incorporated. Scrape the mixture into a large bowl and set aside.

4. Wash and dry the mixer bowl and whisk attachment. Using the stand mixer with the clean bowl and whisk attachment, whisk the egg whites with the remaining ½ cup/100 g sugar on medium-high until stiff peaks form, 3 to 4 minutes. Gently fold half of the dry ingredients into the yolk mixture, and then fold in the remaining dry ingredients. Gently fold in the egg whites just until combined, being careful not to deflate the batter.

5. Fill the éclair cups just a bit more than half full. Bake until springy to the touch and light golden brown, 9 to 12 minutes. Cool in the pan for 1 minute only, and then remove from the pan, using a knife to loosen the sides. Wipe out the pan, oil again, and repeat, using the remaining batter. Cool the cakes completely before filling.

6. TO MAKE THE PUDDING: In a small bowl, whisk the eggs, vanilla, cornstarch, and ½ cup/120 ml of the cream together. Set aside.

7. In a large nonreactive saucepan, combine the granulated sugar, corn syrup, water, and lemon juice and bring to a boil over medium-high heat. Reduce the heat to low and whisk in the molasses, butter, and miso. Simmer for a few minutes, and then add the milk and remaining 1 cup/240 ml cream. Increase the heat to medium, add the egg mixture, and bring back to a boil, whisking vigorously. Reduce the heat to low and continue whisking until the mixture is bubbly and thick, about 5 minutes.

8. Remove the pudding from the heat, and strain through a fine mesh sieve into a glass bowl. Cover the surface directly with plastic wrap to prevent a skin from forming, and let cool at least 30 minutes. (If not using immediately, store the pudding in a covered glass jar for up to 1 week in the refrigerator.)

9. Fill a squirt bottle or piping bag with the pudding. Turn the cakes over and carefully insert the bottle or piping tip into the flat underside of the cake. Squeeze in three equal squirts to distribute the filling evenly. Turn over and sift powdered sugar on top before serving.

MAKES 12 "TWINKIES"

NONG POONSUKWATTNA
NONG'S KHAO MAN GAI

A food cart grows into the new Thai fast food—custom-made and packaged with bravery.

Nong Poonsukwattna's path from Thailand to the top tier of Portland's food scene has been anything but straight. In 2003, at age twenty-three, she set out for America's promised land, with two suitcases, seventy bucks, and a bachelor's degree in business. It didn't buy her much. At first, America looked like a dream. Everything—the cars, the plates, the bacon—was so big. She quickly discovered the nightmare, too. Given her limited English, even 7-Eleven wouldn't hire her. So she spent a couple of years learning the language from television soaps and pop songs while cleaning carpets and being bullied at a Chinese buffet restaurant.

For years, she was mortified to find nothing more than a life of fourteen-hour waitress shifts in Thai-American restaurants dishing out food that tasted nothing like home. Coworkers called her an FOB or "fresh off the boat," scoffing at her notion that customers deserved real Thai food. Who was she to argue? Tables were filled every night. Poonsukwattna gave up everything, even her dog, to hold on to tip money and a goal: to be her own boss in a place that is always happy.

Then, in 2007, she read a newspaper story about Pok Pok, a new chicken shack run by a white guy grilling whole birds, Bangkok style. When she knocked on the door, owner Andy Ricker saw the fire in her eyes, and Nong landed her first cooking job. "He was the first person in America who took me seriously," she recalls. "I had to do a good job. My mother said, 'You are now an ambassador for all the people of Thailand.' It was a lot of pressure."

One year later, inspired by Ricker's authentic grit and playful ambition, Nong imagined her own future in a paper-wrapped bundle of chicken and rice, the food of her youth. She rolled the dice—and $10,000 in savings—on a food cart serving *khao man gai* (pronounced *cow mon guy*), a street-food find rarely seen outside of Thailand. China's Hainan province invented it, Singapore adopted it, Thailand improved it, and, thanks to Nong, Portland owns it. If Oregon had a state dish this would be it: the pioneer spirit seasoned with mad perfection.

Since 2009, Nong's Khao Man Gai has reigned as the star of Portland's grand food-cart experiment. Her colorful little wagon sits on the *Slumdog Millionaire* blocks of downtown Portland, a funkytown of carts crammed together,

inches apart. Steps away, you can find zaftig Polish dumplings from the Old Country or crème brûlée donuts from the modern world, blow-torched to order in the window. Nong blends two schools of hawking into one fresh thought: the old-school Bangkok vendor gambling all on one dish and the new-wave Portland entrepreneur serving food as art and attitude. In Nong's world, techno beats pulse from a windowsill boom box, and *khao man gai* arrives as a ritualistic pleasure, wrapped to order the ancient way, in squares of white butcher paper sealed with a rubber band.

Inside each packet is a tidy mound of jasmine rice, carefully simmered with giant thumbs of ginger and foot-long pandanus leaves in poultry stock until each perfectly moist grain stands defiantly alone. Nong layers on rough-cut chicken, slow-poached until succulent as a peach, plus cucumber slices and a bush of long-stemmed cilantro. Insiders plunk down an extra dollar for fried chicken skin or luscious hunks of liver. As is Thai custom, a cup of delicate broth comes gratis, to keep the throat moist and hungering for more. But the stairway to heaven is the sauce: a deep thrash of ginger, garlic, Thai chiles, fermented soy beans, and Nong's palm sugar syrup. Once you've tasted the whole thing, "It messes with your head," as our food-writing friend Mike Thelin likes to say, unleashing a savage cry from within, taunting your inner Thai food demon, demanding to be fed again and again.

With her plaid hunter's cap and waterfall tattoo tumbling down her right arm, Nong, as everyone calls her, is the humblest cool chick you'll ever meet. Every order passes through her take-out window with that jumbo smile, a gracious bow, and a happy yelp of "thank you, *thank* you," always repeated twice. "She's the most charismatic person in Portland," says barista Tim Roth so emphatically that he sounds like a spokesperson for Travel Oregon, the state's booster organization.

Most Frequently Asked Question at Nong's Khao Man Gai

"Do you have chow mein?"

Nong's cart is the pride of Portland. For years, the burden of impressing a visitor fell on Powell's City of Books, one of the last great independent bookstores, big enough to elect its own mayor. Now it's a straight beeline from the airport to Nong's. Even the great culinary minds are led like sheep. America's food queen Ruth Reichl was squired to Nong's, confidently. Nong is a clutch player. It's like having Kobe Bryant on your team. She's a food assassin. You know you're going to win.

Fast, Cheap, and in Control

After months of searching for an affordable cart, Nong found it: a kettle-corn trailer advertised on Craigslist for $800. In her first negotiation as a business hopeful, the owner added a delivery charge and jacked up the price to $1,000. Then he added a surprise. When she opened the door to her 8-by-8-foot dream, she found stale kettle corn stacked from floor to ceiling and spent her first day as a business owner in America hauling it away. Nong painted her disillusionment in bright colors, adding shades of sunrise yellow, rooster red, and black "because it says serious but fun." The day Nong's Khao Man Gai opened, she cooked seven chickens and was so overwhelmed that a customer came in to help. "I was nervous, scared, on my own," she says. "My heart went boom, boom, boom."

Now Nong's food cart is a model of efficiency, opening at ten a.m. and juggling swarms of customers without even a hint of ruffle. By two p.m. the show is over. Two hundred chicken bundles, gone. The sad news is posted like a ransom note with masking tape and a hand-drawn smiley face: "SOLD OUT! Thank you for your support." Every afternoon, the sign sits cockeyed on a shuttered window next to a heavy padlock protecting Portland's bravest dream.

After two years in the food-cart lane, Nong is thinking big. Her second cart on the Portland State University campus is Trump Tower compared to her Hobbit-size digs blocks away. Nong's V.2 is the springboard for Poonsukwattna's long-simmering dream: to bottle Nong's *khao man gai* sauce and "put a jar in every supermarket in America." These colorfully labeled cylinders hold the concentration of garlic, heat, and heaven that leaves Nong's follower's weak-kneed.

Of course, it hasn't been easy. After paying a food-packaging development company to teach her the ropes, Nong popped a row of sauces in her cart window with knuckle-biting excitement. Two days later, government regulators swooped in with other ideas.

December 20, 2011
Karen:

I've very sorry the sauce has to push back for now. I have an appointment with the health department on Dec 29 to go over the sauce. And we go from there. I'll do whatever it takes. It's just never easy and it's cost a lot of money. But I won't give up.

Thank you very much.

Nong

On weekends, Nong now journeys to Seattle for certification classes. If all goes well, her bottles will be back in business within the year. But this unexpected detour cost her another $5,000. Her eyes grow bigger and blacker as she utters the number. "I'm so fearful of losing everything," she says. "I never want to go back to where I was."

Meanwhile, at long last, Nong is a boss in a happy place. She hired a manager, and three Latino cooks pile into her teeny wagon daily. That means she no longer has to haul thirty-pound jugs of water to the cart herself. What are

employees for, after all? But opening a brick-and-mortar, a long-term goal, would be an even bigger victory. As she puts it: "I wouldn't have to sneak into Nordstrom's bathroom nearby." It's one of many details we never think about when lost in the romance of the food-cart world.

How would life be different if she had opened her cart in Bangkok? Nong reflects on the question. "Maybe I wouldn't have stories in *Men's Health* and on The Food Channel. But I was determined to be a bad ass. Doesn't matter where I am."

NONG'S THAI PICKLED-GARLIC OMELET

One winter night at Robert Reynolds's Chefs Studio—an intimate culinary school by day and a boisterous food salon by night—Nong Poonsukwattna let it be known that her cooking savvy stretched way beyond *khao man gai*, her one-dish wonderment. She wowed a gathering of food-lovers with multiple courses showcasing the elegant, the homey, and the streetwise. But this rich, crisp, savory omelet got the room talking instantly, with bright bursts of mellower-than-expected Thai-style pickled garlic. Serve with rice for breakfast or slice into wedges for a dinner-party snack with a Tamarind Whiskey cocktail (see page 99) from Pok Pok, where Nong found the confidence to cook authentic Thai food in America without the compromises.

3 tbsp coconut or vegetable oil

3 eggs

8 Thai-pickled garlic cloves, peeled and coarsely chopped

1 tbsp freshly squeezed lime juice

1 tsp Golden Mountain Seasoning Sauce

1/2 tsp Thai fish sauce (*nam pla*)

1. In a wok or 10-in/25-mm nonstick skillet, heat the coconut oil over medium-high heat until almost smoking, about 2 minutes.

2. Meanwhile, using a fork, in a large bowl beat the eggs until frothy, 2 to 3 minutes. Stir in the garlic, lime juice, seasoning sauce, and fish sauce. Pour the mixture into the hot oil, swirling the pan to spread the eggs evenly. Let the eggs set without disturbing them, for about 3 minutes. Check the underside to make sure it's crisp and golden brown, and then carefully flip the omelet over. Cook another minute or two and serve hot or at room temperature.

SERVES 2

CHAPTER 4
SUPPER
CLUB
RENEGADES

Communal tables are never-ending dinner parties with some of the best food to be found: boisterous, bountiful, and barely legal.

good as BACON.

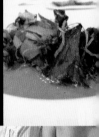

Where Have Neurotics Gone?

NAOMI POMEROY
BEAST

The Ripe supper club leaves behind controversy, an iconoclastic cuisine, and one meat-slinging bad girl juggling communal tables and celebrity status.

Remember the scene in *Gone With the Wind* when a wan, war-haggard Scarlett O'Hara makes a pimped-out plantation gown from green velvet curtains yanked off the walls of her ruined mansion? That's Naomi Pomeroy: a survivor—with style.

Pomeroy grew up in the small town of Corvallis, Oregon, home of the Oregon State Beavers. She attended Portland's Lewis & Clark College but grew up schooled by her single mom, a welfare bohemian who loved all things French. Pomeroy's childhood home channeled Paris *Vogue*, but on the cheap, with thrift-store savvy and broccoli-Cheddar soufflés. Pomeroy was crafty, too. In college, she roomed with five hungry guys and persuaded them to dole out $10 a head for a homemade meal. Instead of doing her homework, she shopped and cooked. She didn't intend to set the table for America's supper-club culture, but that's how the whole thing ignited. "It really started exploding," Pomeroy recalls. "And then I met Michael."

Michael Hebb was an architecture school dropout and self-possessed ideologue in 2001 when he met Pomeroy, a pixie-cut beauty with jet-black hair and ice-blue eyes. They fell in love and launched Ripe, a catering business that operated illegally out of their Northeast Portland bungalow with "fake-it-till-you-make-it" bravado. They liked the name because it implied indulgence, a sense of going too far.

It worked. Ripe gained an instant reputation among the city's well-heeled hip. After barely a year, the duo proclaimed conventional dining a cut-and-paste bore and hatched another idea, e-mailing friends and clients to come for dinner. Just one hitch: Bring a chair and leave it. Another e-mail followed: Come for supper but bring a friend. And always, please leave $5 at the door. Call it a pyramid scheme without the scam. Twice a month, they turned their home into an underground grange hall, endlessly rearranging furniture to accommodate twenty-five dinner guests at a communal table. In the process they defrosted shrimp in their bathtub, hosed dishes on the lawn, and essentially spray-painted their names on Portland's quietly serious food scene like graffiti.

Ripe dinners came with exclusive invites, a giddy taste of danger, and maybe even something meaningful. The curious converged like truth seekers drawn to the fading echoes of a remote Tibetan canyon. A year later, the carpet was ruined, and Hebb and Pomeroy were broke.

But they had stumbled onto a marketing plan for the cyber generation long before anyone had heard of food-cart tweets and Facebook openings. With no start-up costs, Ripe had amassed thousands of followers who signed up for Hebb's seductive Internet alerts and pithy provocations from the food underground.

But with the health department lurking and success looming, the outlaw life was soon over. Under the umbrella of Ripe, they launched Family Supper as a separate entity in a rehabbed industrial building with a real kitchen and a liquor license. "We are expanding our concept into a restaurant, for lack of a better word," Hebb wrote his e-mail army in 2003.

The new Family Supper unfurled in the dark industrial void of North Portland, past a chain-link fence and down an alley lined with trash cans. There was a door but no sign, no street number—begging the question: If I go in, will they let me out? Inside, the minimalist room looked like an art gallery, except there was no art. Just three long tables meticulously set and forty strangers drifting in and about like characters in a Robert Altman movie, sipping Cutty Sark. In the corner kitchen, T-shirt-clad Tommy Habetz—a Portland newcomer still bristling with the DNA of his New York mentor, Italian food lord Mario Batali—worked over a vat of chicken liver ragu.

"Welcome," shouted Hebb, the cool cult leader. "Our menu tonight includes cavalo nero, a black kale that just started growing in this country. We pulled it up today. I think our chef makes the best pasta in the world. Help yourself to dessert. Everything is on the honor system, including money."

With this, platters of transcendent food were passed hand to hand, candles flickered, music twinkled, family secrets were spilled to new table neighbors—and the game changed, forever.

In 2004, Ripe added another charm to its bracelet, a more "traditional" restaurant without e-mail invites or communal seats. Clarklewis, rising out of the bleakness of Water Avenue next to the train tracks, looked unlike any restaurant anywhere: a 1910 loading dock transformed into a setting of industrial neorealism with sophisticated peasant cooking crackling over a wood fire. Fresh-whacked legs of lamb and chicory salads with house-cured pancetta hung out alongside chipped paint and art glass in a room as dark as a planetarium. Customers read menus by flashlight, amusing some, infuriating others. Chef Morgan Brownlow, a skateboard dude and gifted teenage understudy of salami god Paul Bertolli at San Francisco's Oliveto, wheeled gargantuan pigs right through the dining room, startling customers accustomed to shrink-wrapped supermarket pork chops. Years before Portland embraced meat as a religion, Brownlow was an apostle, butchering whole animals right in the open kitchen and using every bit, causing gleeful exclamations from Hebb, such as "Of course that's delicious; it's from a pig's ass."

"The first time I went to Clarklewis, it was magic," says Toro Bravo mastermind John Gorham. "I saw the imagination. They were having fun, a party. I thought: 'That's what I want to do. It doesn't have to be stuffy.'"

Hebb and Pomeroy quickly captured the attention of glitz mongers, business minds, and investors ready to bank on the couple W magazine called "the prince and princess of the Pacific Northwest food scene." But the threads started to unravel with a third child: the Gotham Building Tavern, born in 2005 with a slick Lincoln Log design and $50 cover charges for two floor-to-ceiling wooden dining "cages." After a year of backlash and confusion, GBT went down in Portland history as a disaster movie starring major kitchen talent: Habetz, Pomeroy, and an unknown Gabriel Rucker.

Through it all, Ripe courted controversy merrily and fueled the gossip mill endlessly. It electrified Portland and divided Portland. It found beauty in ugly places, and created a new community of hybrids: cooks, customers, waiters, and local artists, all in it together. It put a rising independent food scene on the national food map, and unearthed a generation of talents who went on to build Stumptown's thriving food culture. Ripe gave a face to an emerging Portland style—communal, intentional, crafty—and made diners feel that eating out could provide much more than sustenance.

Then it slammed like a Portland windstorm into financial and marital ruin in 2006, leaving a slew of angry cooks, farm vendors, and investors at the altar. A sign in the window provided the epitaph for Portland's DIY dreamers: "Michael has left the Gotham Building."

Pomeroy? Like Scarlett emerging from the wreckage of Tara, she surveyed the scorched landscape and said,

"Tomorrow is another day." In 2007, the woman who had taken a backseat to a charismatic husband and two culinary hotshots rose from the ashes and unleashed Beast: full-length nights of animal fever, communal eating, and feminine cool in a transitioning Northeast neighborhood. The kitchen makes all the decisions for you: set menu, set prices, and "substitutions politely declined." On Sunday mornings, that can mean dessert to start—sugar-dusted cherry clafoutis—and Pomeroy's extreme chocolate truffle cake to end. Within a year, Beast roared mightily, as one girl (and her foxy sous chef) challenged Portland's meat-slaying bad boys with pig love and Paris-on-a-budget charm.

Beast is a new kind of supper club: a dinner party with reservations and Otis Redding. The tiny room takes cues from a graffiti-like wall chalk-marked with recipes, farmer phone lists, and wisdom from Pythagoras and Tom Waits not to mention Miss Piggy, plus ecstatic proclamations like "Praise the lard!" Pomeroy's elegantly porky pot pies and creamy root soups are more likely to nurture you into a blissful food coma than start a food revolution. Mostly, she digs deep into French soul food and Oregon's sustainability ethos in dishes brandishing feminine charm and a bone saw of meat. Think Julia Child on a blind date with Anthony Bourdain.

Beast is all heart and gut, seasoned with sweat, integrity, and deep incursions into Portland's farmers' market. Pomeroy gets graceful with foie foie bonbons, a house signature, but she likes her he-man foods, too, including short-rib hash and hollandaise to greet a Sunday morning. There's no mistaking the hand, the sense of food imagined by a gal who loves long earrings and high heels. But unfasten your seat belt; that ramp-stuffed saddle of rabbit dressed in beurre blanc is merely the third hop on a long road trip.

The Next Battlefields: *Iron Chef* and *Top Chef Masters*

Never count out Naomi Pomeroy, that's the thing. Doesn't matter that she's never worked the line or met an immersion machine. No matter that she opened her sexy rock 'n' roll bistro with no money, no stove, and everything on the DL, skirting codes.

Just ask Philly's Latin-fusion master José Garces, owner of a gazillion restaurants and multiple awards. Garces may

have bested Pomeroy on *Iron Chef America* in 2010 but only by a few truffle shavings. Doesn't matter that the cameras caught the hands of her twenty-five-year-old collaborator Mika Paredes trembling like Mount St. Helens on eruption day and exclaiming over boiled milk, "Oh! Goodness!" While Garces scored on "originality" and "plating," team Beast crushed him in the only category that truly counts, "taste."

Or ask the eight *Top Chef Masters* who packed up their knives on Season 3 as the younger, less experienced Pomeroy stayed alive, slashing her way to fourth place and raising her reputation as one of America's rising female chefs.

How did Pomeroy do it? By going into the belly of Beast, keeping it real, Portland style, with food that keeps you licking your chops days later. A battalion of contemporary dishes trying too hard are little match for bone-warming beef Wellingtons and porcini-braised chicken thighs. But culinary game shows also thrive on survivor skills, the ability to deliver in extreme situations, and Pomeroy is a pro. That's her secret weapon, though the killer shade of lipstick didn't hurt.

"All that crazy stuff Michael and I did made me a fierce competitor," says Pomeroy. "Making gourmet meals in a dorm room or rinsing pasta in the shower—that doesn't even phase me. Most of these chefs come from well-equipped kitchens, with every ingredient you ever wanted. Growing up, I never had anything. I was always the scrappy one."

Which doesn't mean that the experience wasn't traumatic. "The pressure was intense," Pomeroy confessed before *Top Chef Masters* aired in 2011. "Ninety-eight percent of the time, you're sure you were going to puke. We all have PTSD. For weeks after taping, I didn't have one dream that wasn't *Master Chef.* I'm still recovering. It was a roller coaster."

Beauty and the Beast

Back at Beast after spring's television whirl is another reality show: sixty-four guests and fourteen-hour days, four nights a week. Pomeroy and Paredes, her trusted aide-de-camp and "kitchen wife" compose plates at a prep station that doubles as the stage for this two-woman show. Tonight's feast, decidedly anti-Beast, is vegetarian, part of a new monthly dining series that sells out in hours. Could this be a new direction? After all, Porklandia is under siege from a meat-free crowd that is vocal and growing. Pomeroy confesses she was once a vegetarian, coughing up this surprise: "When I go out, I'm not looking to eat a bunch of meat." Will Beast transition into a vegetable-loving beauty? Or do bigger fish loom on the horizon?

"I'm open to seeing what the universe brings. That's how it works for me," says Pomeroy, who now fields offers and makes public appearances routinely. "I've gone through a lot in the last six years. Today is the six-year anniversary of the opening of the Gotham. I've succeeded, failed, succeeded again. I've never been a planner. I've never had an expectation of being successful. That's not how I roll. I'm very in the moment with my stuff. It's the hog I've got to take down today. That's how it works, even my menus. It's just whatever I see in the morning."

Naomi Pomeroy's Table

Say it with demi-glace: "I include this on every menu. It's the ultimate meat sauce; acid, fat, truffle salt, thirty-year-balsamic, all at once. It's real sexy but also manly, like putting meat into liquid form on the plate."

Think simple: "Big, long, dark wood tables. Candles. Good wine glasses. Name a time when that isn't beautiful."

MAPLE-SUGARED PORK BELLY ON TOAST WITH FAVA BEANS AND PICKLED GREEN STRAWBERRIES

Back in Portland after carving her initials in America's food landscape as a savvy player on *Top Chef Masters 3*, Naomi Pomeroy went on a recipe rampage and then quickly proclaimed, "This is it, the *best* thing Beast has ever served." Who can argue with the queen of the pig? This rich, sweet-sour show-stopper puts lip-smacking pork belly at the center of conversation, with shouts and murmurs scattered all around. The final touches include sautéed fava beans; thick slices of buttered toast; green strawberry pickles; and two Pomeroy signatures, herbaceous salsa verde and, for a last bellow from the mountaintops, an indulgent demi-glace. (Don't tell Pomeroy, but we skipped the demi-glace and simply reduced the braising liquid, and the dish was still richer than Carlos Slim. Make your own demi-glace if you must, or buy it from a specialty market.) The whole thing looks rather daunting but only requires a couple of hours of prep time over two days, and then time spent assembling the parts. The real secret is flexibility. Think like a chef: Use what you have and what's in season. Asparagus, green beans, or snap peas can stand in for the favas; pasta can replace the toast; and radishes, small turnips, or cherries can sub for the green strawberries. Day One: Season, sear, and braise the pork belly, and pickle the strawberries. Day Two: Reduce the braising liquid, cook the favas, make the salsa verde, and assemble. Piece of cake, or, even better, pork.

One 3-lb/1.4-kg slab pork belly, skin removed

Fine sea salt and freshly ground black pepper

1¼ cups/250 g maple or muscavado sugar

8 tbsp/120 ml olive oil

1 large sweet onion, coarsely chopped

2 carrots, coarsely chopped

2 celery stalks, coarsely chopped

1 small leek, white and pale green parts only, coarsely chopped

6 cups/1.4 L chicken or beef stock, or salted water, warmed

1 cup/240 ml dry white wine

1 head garlic, halved crosswise

4 sprigs fresh thyme

1½ lb/680 g whole fava beans in the pod

½ cup/120 ml good-quality sherry vinegar

8 slices country bread, toasted and lightly buttered

½ cup/120 ml homemade or store-bought demi-glace (optional)

½ cup/120 ml Beast's Salsa Verde (page 126)

1 cup/225 g Naomi Pomeroy's Pickled Green Strawberries (page 127)

1. Preheat the oven to 325°F/165°C/gas 3.

2. Using a sharp knife, score the fatty side of the pork belly with crosshatch marks 1 in/2.5 cm apart and ⅟₁₆ in/2 mm deep. Rub 2 tsp sea salt and several grindings of pepper all over the belly.

3. Heat a Dutch oven over high heat to almost smoking. (If your pot isn't large enough, you can cut the belly in half and sear in two batches.) Lower the heat to medium and sear the belly on the fatty side until nicely browned, 8 to 10 minutes. Turn and brown the other side for a few minutes. Transfer to a baking sheet to cool slightly. Rub ¼ cup/50 g of the maple sugar over the belly.

4. In the same pan, warm 4 tbsp/60 ml of the olive oil over medium-high heat. Add the onion, carrots, and celery and sauté, stirring occasionally, until lightly colored, about 10 minutes. Add the leek and 1 tsp salt and sauté another minute. Place the pork belly in the pan, meat-side down. Add the stock, wine, garlic, and thyme, making sure the liquid just covers the meat (adding more if necessary).

5. Place a sheet of parchment paper over the belly, then cover the pan very tightly with aluminum foil. Braise in the oven until fork-tender, 3 to 4 hours. Remove from the oven, and carefully lift off the foil and paper (take care to avoid the hot steam that will be released). Cool the belly completely in the braising liquid, 2½ to 3 hours.

6. Transfer the meat to a large plate. Cover and refrigerate until cold enough to cut without causing it to fall apart, at least 4 hours or overnight. Strain the braising liquid into a bowl, pressing down on the vegetables to release their juices; cover and refrigerate.

7. An hour before serving, preheat the oven to 425°F/ 220°C/gas 7.

8. Remove the braising liquid and pork belly from the refrigerator. Discard the vegetables. Cut the cold belly into eight 3-in/7.5-mm squares; set aside. Skim the solid layer of fat from the surface of the braising liquid and discard the fat. Measure out 1 cup/240 ml liquid (in which to reheat the pork), and set aside.

9. (If you're not using a demi-glace for the finishing sauce, reduce the remaining braising liquid in a small saucepan. Over medium-high heat, boil the braising liquid, stirring occasionally, until reduced to about 2 cups/480 ml and slightly thickened, about 15 minutes. Season with salt and pepper, and keep the sauce warm.)

10. Remove the fava beans from their pods. Bring a small pot of lightly salted water to a boil. Blanch the fava beans until just tender, 3 to 4 minutes. Transfer to a bowl of ice water to cool. Peel the favas and set aside. (If the favas are very young, skip the peeling step.)

11. In a small saucepan over medium heat, combine the vinegar and remaining 1 cup/200 g maple sugar, stirring often, to make a glaze, about 2 minutes.

12. Heat 2 tbsp of the olive oil in a large ovenproof skillet over medium-high heat, and place the pieces of pork belly meat-side down in the pan. Brush the sweet vinegar glaze over the tops and sides of the pork, and then turn off the heat. Pour the reserved braising liquid into the skillet with the pork belly. Roast in the oven until the pork is warmed all the way through and the sauce is bubbling, 10 to 15 minutes.

13. While the pork is roasting, heat the remaining 2 tbsp olive oil in a small saucepan over low heat and stir in the favas and a healthy pinch of salt. Cook them gently, stirring, until tender, 3 to 5 minutes.

14. Place one slice of toast in each of eight wide, shallow serving bowls. Top each with one piece of pork belly, and ladle on about 2 tbsp of the demi-glace or ¼ cup/60 ml of the reduced braising liquid. Top with a spoonful of salsa verde, then scatter a handful of favas and a few pickled strawberries around the bowl. Serve immediately.

SERVES 8

BEAST'S SALSA VERDE

One way you know you're eating at Naomi Pomeroy's communal table: a thick, chunky, heady herbal "salad" rests like a celebratory crown over everything and anything, root soups to elegant meats.

1 medium shallot, finely chopped

2 tbsp aged white wine vinegar, plus more if needed

½ tsp fine sea salt, plus more if needed

¼ cup/15 g finely chopped fresh Italian flat-leaf parsley

Heaping 1 tbsp finely chopped fresh mint

Heaping 1 tbsp finely chopped fresh chervil

Heaping 1 tbsp finely chopped fresh chives

½ cup/120 ml extra-virgin olive oil

Lemon-infused olive oil

In a small bowl, combine the shallot, vinegar, and salt. In a medium bowl, combine the parsley, mint, chervil, and chives and add enough of the extra-virgin oil to cover. Just before serving, stir in the vinegar mixture and drizzle in the lemon oil to taste. Taste and add vinegar and salt, if needed. The salsa is best served fresh, although it keeps for up to 2 days if refrigerated.

MAKES APPROXIMATELY ¾ CUP/180 ML

NAOMI POMEROY'S PICKLED GREEN STRAWBERRIES

Portland chefs have a new spring fling: unripe Granny Smith–colored strawberries freckled with pale brown seeds. Unlike their juicy-sweet ruby-red siblings, these berries are more vegetal, with a pale fruit flavor matched by a delicate tartness. Beast transforms these seasonal gems into unexpected pickles to scatter over rich meats or cheese plates, complete with edible hull, or to garnish a house salad of arugula, sweet red strawberries, and shaved Humboldt Fog cheese. If you can't find green strawberries, worry not; Pomeroy's spice-forward, liqueur-splashed formula is but a playground for a number of worthy subjects: unpitted cherries, apples, rhubarb, asparagus, or even radishes.

1 tbsp coriander seeds

1 tbsp fennel seeds

1 tsp allspice seeds

½ tsp anise seeds

1 whole clove

½ cinnamon stick

1 tbsp fennel pollen

½ tsp chile flakes

1 small bay leaf

6 cups/1.4 L water

2 cups/480 ml aged sweet sauvignon blanc vinegar

1½ cups/300 g sugar

6 tbsp/110 g fine sea salt

¼ cup/60 ml honey

¼ cup/60 ml Cointreau liqueur

¼ cup/60 ml crème de framboise liqueur

4 cups/575 g whole green strawberries, cherries, or radishes (see headnote)

1. In a large dry skillet over medium heat, toast the coriander seeds, fennel seeds, allspice seeds, anise seeds, clove, and cinnamon stick for a few minutes, shaking the pan to stir. Transfer the spices to a bowl and toss in the fennel pollen, chile flakes, and bay leaf. Cut a large square of cheesecloth, and place the spices in the center. Bring the four corners up and together and twist them in order to tie a knot to enclose the sachet.

2. Put the sachet in a medium saucepan. Add the water, vinegar, sugar, salt, honey, and both liqueurs and bring to a boil over medium-high heat. Boil for 5 minutes, then turn off the heat.

3. Place the strawberries in a large, glass jar. Pour in enough of the hot liquid to cover. Cool to room temperature to use right away, or cover the jar with a lid and refrigerate for up to 2 weeks.

MAKES 1 QT/450 G

COURTNEY SPROULE
DIN DIN SUPPER CLUB

A roving kitchen imagines theatrical tables and culinary adventure in challenging places.

It's not every day that you eat twenty-three miniature dishes, over four hours, with fourteen strangers at one grandiose table in the middle of a 1920s funeral parlor reborn as a music hall. Or swoon over squab primed by cream and blackcap raspberries while watching a weary band of beach-stranded studs battle a giant mutant crab (thanks to 1961's *Mysterious Island* projected on the wall). Or conclude a theatrical meal rolled out in nine acts with cognac and chocolates while playing pool in an outdoor rec room. All this while a DJ spins soul on old wax at levels loud enough to wake the dead.

Then again, Din Din Supper Club is not an everyday dining experience. Courtney Sproule has imagined a roving culinary adventure for the times: fine dining without the starch, to say the least. This is serious eating, meticulously farm-sourced and theatrically art-directed in changing locations to tempt, amuse, and delight while challenging the boundaries of your comfort zone.

E-mail invites only hint at mysteries to come: brunches attended to by skateboarding waiters, musicians playing on tabletops, and food-focused nights in vacant lofts. Or, in the case of that twenty-three–dish blowout, games of culinary scale with sky-high candelabras and giant monster cinema set against teeny dishes on teeny plates; even the menu arrived in tiny type, its petite indulgences revealed only through magnifying glasses, as Sproule reminds us to appreciate the small in a world increasingly too big.

Bites, Cameras, Action!

Courtney Sproule approaches meals as Werner Herzog directs a film: like an active volcano, stopping at nothing to get the details right, and always in unthinkable terrain. The North Carolina native cooks in alleyways, former church basements, and farm fields, mounting intricate meals without the luxury of dishwashers or, sometimes, running water. At 2010's Sea in the City supper, diners ate like seafaring fools among sea fans, pearls, and hand-burned messages in bottles, while twenty-nine-year-old Sproule attended to fresh clams and homemade pasta strewn on office tables lined with butcher paper. No two menus are alike, and no obstacle is too great for her crew of artists, musicians, and off-duty line cooks who love the action.

"I'll go anywhere," says Sproule. "A nontraditional space can be an advantage in pulling off something special. I want people to feel part of something that happens only once, within those walls, with those people."

On one Valentine's Day, she arrived at an art gallery in a yellow-belted black vintage dress, ready to stage three nights of sexy Din Dins "for the stag ladies and boys," only to discover that the prep room no longer existed. "No sink, no refrigeration, nothing," recalls Sproule. "It was intense. I had planned all these luscious custards and technique-driven dishes. We had to set up right in the corner. I'm thinking, 'Seared foie gras with beurre rouge! How the hell am I going to do that?' We put three tubs out back as coolers. It was pouring, chilled-to-the-bone cold. It was February in Portland, Oregon. I was soaked."

Outside in the rain, the sorbet machine croaked along with Din Din's plan to churn icy wonders to order. Working only with her traveling Bunsen burners and rented convection oven, Sproule still fired up a meal to steal hearts: beautiful *gougères* throwing unexpected whiffs of blue cheese and orange blossom water; steamy mussels cradling silky sabayon custard; wonderfully unruly greens from a Bend farm; and, finally, the sweet smell of success, homemade rosewater caramels, orange truffles, and wine from Gascony all around.

Parting Thoughts

April 2011
Hi Karen,

Your question about why the hell I take on these crazy endeavors is a really good one! It got me thinking!

It comes down to what really intrigues me about food. It's so basic to our survival, in the animalistic sense, but also incredibly cultural and very distinctly human. I think that's why we gather around food. It's humble common ground and also a platform for creativity and expression. din din in some ways is a very exaggerated version of that idea.

Does that make any sense?
—court

Totally.

Din Din's Do-It-Yourself Supper Club

In the beginning, Courtney Sproule just wanted to show the beauty of the table to "people used to getting a burrito and moving on." But Din Din grew into one woman's idea of the perfect dinner party—extremely personal and intimate but for strangers. The food and mood may change, but the formula remains.

Start with a theme: Build around an ingredient, a holiday, or even a pop-culture icon. The fun is as important as the food.

Set a mysterious tone: Supper clubs run on e-mail teases—a few clever words, a touch of mystery, and just enough detail to get appetites revved and imaginations roaming.

Hand out props immediately: Everyone looks better with a glass of something, anything, in their hands. Get sips and snacks going, pronto, and watch the conversation flow.

Embrace the little details: Every plate, every tabletop, every moment should be considered with one question in mind—What will make guests feel special? That's the Din Din mode. "It's serving soup from your grandma's antique pitcher, throwing a backyard buffet on a camping tarp set with beautiful china, showing people the rewards of spending the entire evening at the table."

GREEN GARLIC SOUP WITH SAVORY PAIN PERDU AND STEAMED MUSSELS

Courtney Sproule may cook on wandering burners in make-shift spaces, but nothing is impromptu about her recipes. This is food lovers' all-day cooking founded on French technique (and mentor Robert Reynolds's philosophies) but going its own mad way with flavor combinations never imagined, and an insistence on finely chopping even a parsley stem "on the bias." Organization is the key to this theatrical spring soup. Each bowl is lined with brandied French toast, then topped with fresh herbs and steamed mussels. And that's before the soup even makes an appearance. (Actually, it's more of a glorified sauce, poured table-side from a fancy pitcher.) Green garlic, a taste of pure spring, mild and grassy, pops up fleet-ingly at farmers' markets; as an alternative, substitute leeks mixed with a couple of garlic cloves. Have all the ingredients ready, as assembly is quick once the ball starts rolling.

Soup

2 tsp extra-virgin olive oil

1 cup/225 g thinly sliced green garlic (white and pale green portions), or 2 leeks and 2 garlic cloves, thinly sliced

1½ tsp fine sea salt

Heaping 1 tbsp fresh thyme leaves

2 cups/480 ml good-quality chicken stock, warmed

1 to 2 tsp Banyuls or sherry wine vinegar

Pinch of nutmeg

¾ tsp ground coriander

1 tbsp crème fraîche

Pain Perdu

5 eggs

1½ cups/355 ml half-and-half

1½ tsp fine sea salt

1 tbsp sugar

¾ tsp *quatre épices* (or a pinch each of ground white pepper, nutmeg, ginger, and clove)

3 tbsp good-quality brandy

2 tsp unsalted butter

Three ¾-in-/2-cm-thick slices brioche

Mussels

½ cup/120 ml white wine

5 sprigs fresh thyme

5 fresh parsley stems, finely chopped on the bias (diagonally)

1 large bay leaf

1 medium shallot, finely chopped

1¼ lb/570 g small mussels, scrubbed and de-bearded

1 handful fresh Italian parsley, finely chopped, for garnish

1 handful fresh blood sorrel, finely chopped, for garnish

1 handful fresh chives, finely chopped, for garnish

continued

1. TO MAKE THE SOUP: In a medium saucepan, warm the olive oil over medium-low heat. Add the green garlic and ½ tsp of the salt and reduce the heat to low. Cover and cook, stirring occasionally, until the vegetables are completely soft and sweet, about 15 minutes, adding a little water if they begin to brown. Add the thyme leaves, and cook another few minutes.

2. Pour ½ cup/120 ml of the chicken stock into the pan, and then scrape the mixture into a blender. Blend on high, holding down the lid, for a minute or so, then add the remaining stock and blend until the soup has the consistency of heavy cream. Add the vinegar, nutmeg, coriander, crème fraîche, and the remaining 1 tsp salt and purée until blended. Season with a dash of vinegar, if necessary. Set aside.

3. TO MAKE THE PAIN PERDU: Preheat the oven to 375°F/190°C/gas 5.

4. In the bowl of a stand mixer fitted with the whisk attachment, combine the eggs, half-and-half, salt, sugar, *quatre épices*, and brandy. Whisk on high speed until frothy, about 5 minutes. Pour the egg mixture into a shallow baking dish.

5. In a large skillet over medium heat, melt the butter, taking care not to let it burn. Meanwhile, quickly soak a brioche slice in the egg mixture for 30 seconds per side (enough time to absorb the liquid). Immediately place the brioche in the skillet, and cook until golden brown, about 2 minutes per side. Repeat for the remaining two brioche slices.

6. Transfer the brioche slices to a baking sheet and bake until the custard is just slightly set in the center and the brioche is puffed up, 5 to 8 minutes. Remove from the oven. Cut each slice in half diagonally. Place six soup bowls in the oven to warm.

7. TO COOK THE MUSSELS: Combine the wine, thyme, parsley stems, bay leaf, and shallot in a medium saucepan. Arrange the mussels in a single layer in the pan, cover, and bring to a boil over high heat. (Peek inside to see if it's boiling.) Immediately reduce the heat to medium-high and shake the pan or gently stir with a large spoon. Cook, covered, until the mussels begin to open, 3 to 4 minutes. Remove the mussels as they open (discard any that do not open).

8. Warm up the soup in a small saucepan over medium-low heat. Transfer the hot soup to a warm ceramic pitcher. In a small bowl, toss the chopped parsley, sorrel, and chives to combine. Place one triangle of brioche in the center of each warmed bowl, sprinkle with a heaping 1 tbsp of the mixed herbs, then top each with four or five mussels. At the table, carefully pour a little soup into the bowls around the pain perdu and serve.

SERVES 6

LAMB CHOPS WITH MERGUEZ SAUSAGE AND PICKLED BLUEBERRIES

The heart and the bones of Din Din are perfectly expressed here: juicy chops, beautifully seared and tiered with surprise. Creamed onions thick with thyme leaves and crushed coriander accompany the meat, along with the bold accent of pickled blueberries, wild mushrooms, and spicy lamb sausage all sizzled up and spooned on top. Make the blueberries in advance for organizational sanity, and pre-salt the lamb the day before for super-tenderness.

Lamb Chops

Six 6-oz/170-g bone-in lamb chops, at room temperature

1 tbsp coarse sea salt

1 tbsp extra-virgin olive oil

Onions

1 tbsp extra-virgin olive oil

3 small onions, thinly sliced

1 tsp fine sea salt

1 cup/240 ml good-quality chicken stock

1¼ tsp coriander seeds, gently crushed

1 tbsp fresh thyme leaves

¼ cup/60 ml heavy cream

Zest of ½ lemon

Sausage

1 tsp olive oil

5 oz/140 g merguez sausage links, cut on the bias into ¼-in-/6-mm-thick slices

8 oz/225 g wild mushrooms, cut into ¼-in-/6-mm-thick slices

½ tsp fine sea salt

6 sprigs fresh savory, chopped

2 small garlic cloves, mashed

6 tbsp/85 g drained Din Din's Pickled Blueberries (page 134)

Piment d'Espellette, for dusting

1. TO PREPARE THE LAMB CHOPS: One day before cooking, place the lamb chops on a rack over a baking sheet and season both sides with a generous ½ tsp coarse salt per chop, pressing the crystals into the flesh. Refrigerate uncovered (to dry-age the meat) for 24 hours. Bring to room temperature for 1 hour before cooking.

2. In a large heavy skillet, heat the olive oil over high heat. Sear the lamb chops to brown evenly, about 3 minutes per side. Transfer to a baking sheet and set aside. Let the skillet cool for a few minutes.

3. TO PREPARE THE ONIONS: Add the olive oil to the lamb fat remaining in the skillet and heat over medium-low heat until hot. Add the onions and ½ tsp of the fine sea salt and reduce the heat to low. Cover with a tight-fitting lid and cook gently without browning until the onions are soft and sweet, about 30 minutes.

4. Stir the stock and coriander into the skillet, raise the heat to medium, and bring to a boil. Reduce the heat to low and simmer gently until the onions are glazed, about 15 minutes. Stir in the thyme and cream and simmer until the onions have just absorbed the cream, another few minutes. Remove from the heat and stir in the lemon zest and remaining ½ tsp salt. Set aside in a warm place.

5. Preheat the oven to 450°F/230°C/gas 8.

continued

6. TO COOK THE SAUSAGE: In a medium skillet over medium-low heat, warm the olive oil until hot. Add the sliced sausage and cook, turning the slices over after 1 to 2 minutes, until just cooked through, about 3 minutes. Using a slotted spoon or tongs, transfer the sausage to a bowl, leaving the fat in the pan.

7. Add the mushrooms and salt to the skillet and cover. Cook over medium-low heat, stirring occasionally, until the mushrooms give up their liquid, about 15 minutes. Uncover and continue cooking on low, stirring, until the mushrooms are nicely browned and dry, about 15 minutes. Stir in the chopped savory, garlic, pickled blueberries, and cooked sausage, and cook 1 minute more.

8. Roast the chops in the oven until medium-rare, about 5 minutes, depending on the meat's thickness or until a meat thermometer reaches 135°F/57°C. Remove from the oven, and transfer to a platter. Cover with a kitchen towel and let rest for 5 minutes.

9. Gently reheat the onions and sausage mixtures in two separate pans. Spoon an equal amount of the onion mixture onto each of six warm plates. Top with a lamb chop and some of the sausage-mushroom mixture. Dust with *piment d'Espellette* and serve.

SERVES 6

DIN DIN'S PICKLED BLUEBERRIES

Finding the right condiment to kick up meat is a higher calling. It must be manly but stylish, accessible but slightly dangerous. These bold blues are it: bright, clear, and frontal. Spoon alongside cured meats, or chop them into a relish to give a surprising lift to a grilled bratwurst.

½ cup/120 ml Banyuls or sherry wine vinegar

½ cup/120 ml white vinegar

½ cup/100 g sugar

2 tbsp kosher salt

1 garlic clove, thinly sliced

½ tsp coriander seed

2 sprigs fresh savory

2 thick strips lemon zest

2 small shallots, thinly sliced

1 cup/150 g fresh or dried blueberries

1. In a medium saucepan, combine both vinegars, the sugar, salt, garlic, coriander seed, savory, lemon zest, and shallots. Bring to a boil over medium-high heat, stirring to dissolve the sugar, and remove from the heat.

2. *If using fresh berries* Place the blueberries in a small mason jar. Pour in the hot liquid, cover loosely, and steep for an hour at room temperature.

If using dried berries Add the berries to the pan and stir. Simmer gently over low heat until softened, about 5 minutes. Pour the berries and liquid into a small mason jar, cover loosely, and steep for an hour at room temperature.

3. Use immediately, or tighten the lid and refrigerate up to 3 days.

MAKES 1 CUP/225 G

HAZELNUT PANNA COTTA WITH PINOT NOIR STRAWBERRIES

Every restaurant, it seems, serves *panna cotta* or "cooked cream," but none does it like this, intensely flavorful and so light you fear it might levitate off the plate. Things really get interesting when the hazelnut flavor hits—a golden brown haze of nutty particles free floating on top. Oregon is the world's hazelnut headquarters, and the best come from Freddy Guys, a Portland farmers' market favorite with a website boasting "Read about us in the *New York Times*!" Grab them if you can. Break out some pinot noir for dinner, and let guests macerate their berries at the table to spoon over dessert: very French, very Din Din.

Panna Cotta

½ tsp vegetable oil

½ cup/70 g raw hazelnuts

½ vanilla bean

¾ cup/180 ml whole milk

1 cup/240 ml heavy cream

3 tbsp plus 1 tsp sugar

¼ tsp kosher salt

1 tsp unflavored gelatin

2 tbsp cold water

2 tsp good brandy

Strawberries

2 to 3 tsp sugar

½ cup/120 ml Oregon pinot noir

8 ripe strawberries, cut into ¼-in-/6-mm-thick slices

1. TO MAKE THE PANNA COTTA: Coat six 2- to 3-oz/60- to 90-ml ramekins with the vegetable oil and set aside.

2. Preheat the oven to 375°F/190°C/gas 5. Place the hazelnuts on a baking sheet and toast, watching carefully to avoid burning them, until lightly browned and fragrant, 8 to 10 minutes. Cool briefly, then enclose the nuts in a kitchen towel. Using your hands, rub the nuts together to remove their skins. Set the nuts aside.

3. Halve the vanilla bean lengthwise, and, using the dull side of a knife, scrape the seeds into a medium saucepan. Add the vanilla bean pod, hazelnuts, milk, cream, sugar, and salt. Bring to a boil over medium-high heat, and then immediately remove from the heat. Discard the vanilla pod.

4. While still hot, transfer the mixture to a blender and, holding the lid down, pulse about four times to break up the nuts slightly. Return the mixture to the same pot to infuse at room temperature, about 15 minutes.

5. Put the gelatin in a large bowl and sprinkle the cold water over it to moisten. Set aside.

6. Over medium heat, warm the hazelnut mixture until just hot to the touch and starting to steam, about 3 minutes. Add the brandy and immediately remove from the heat. Strain the mixture through a fine-mesh sieve into the bowl of gelatin, whisking well to combine. Strain one more time over a clean bowl. Pour into the prepped ramekins, and cover loosely with plastic wrap. Chill for 4 to 6 hours, until set.

7. FOR THE STRAWBERRIES: In a medium bowl, whisk the sugar and wine together. Add the strawberries and marinate until they've softened slightly and absorbed some of the wine, about 20 minutes.

8. Remove the panna cotta from the ramekins by running a hot knife around the inside edge. Turn each upside down over a separate serving plate and tap the ramekin to release. Garnish each with a few spoonfuls of the strawberries and their liquid. Serve immediately.

SERVES 6

YIANNI DOULIS
WILD GOOSE FARM

The chickens come home to roost at a wildlife refuge and urban ag speakeasy.

June in Portland: Your skin is the color of skim milk; it's been *that* long since it saw the sun. The skies bulge with clouds as cheerful as gray flannel suits. You call this summer? What is one to do? Bundle up in sweaters and don sunglasses, optimistically and spitefully, then head outdoors to do what Portlanders do: eat and drink like lucky fools and bitch about the weather. And all the better in a clandestine setting. This is what sixty-five hopeful strangers had in mind one chilly afternoon sitting in a farm field—coats, shades, and all—to savor the freshest food to be found, farm picked, just butchered, and wood-fired only steps away.

Wild Goose Farm is the new rural food experience: raw, intimate, and unscripted yet elegant and meticulously crafted. This charming, slightly scraggly farm on Sauvie Island is deep in lush grass and surrounded by garden patches, beehives, chicken coops, and a big barn kitchen. The linen is starchily pressed, and the liquors are handmade, but no one bothers to hide the compost heap.

Sauvie Island is a spacious parcel of paradise where spellbinding aviation formations swoop over dreamy farm plots just fifteen minutes from downtown Portland. At bountiful U-pick berry fields, giddy locals stuff buckets with world-class strawberries, thumb-size marionberries, and the finest raspberries on the planet. On the island, you can cut-your-own Christmas tree, pluck pumpkins from sprawling patches, snap peaches off trees, or snip flowers from fields of blazing colors, all for a song. Some folks come for fine bird watching; others head straight for the nude beach.

Sauvie Island is also a wildlife refuge for great blue herons, wood ducks, and urban dwellers reinventing themselves. When he plotted a midlife revamp in 2009, eco-architect Yianni Doulis didn't need his Harvard degree to comprehend Portland's sagging development prospects. With his interior designer wife, Jessica Helgerson, he grabbed a rare island vacancy and turned a childhood fantasy of log cabin life into a little house on the prairie fit for Tom Sawyer and Martha Stewart. Doulis immersed himself in cheese-making experiments and the salumi arts while building his food dream: an Italian wood oven, rising as big as an igloo from his free-ranging front yard. They imagined Wild Goose Farm as a destination for eating close to the source, with celebratory family dinners unfolding over hours, days even, like meals in the Europe of their childhoods. They planted

rows of vegetables, four kinds of potatoes, and a food lover's fantasy of currants, quince, and mulberries next to tree houses and ladders poking into fruit trees. Meanwhile, Doulis sketched plans for workshops and a tiny farm stand with "site-made provisions" and just-hatched eggs.

In 2011, their ag-urban dream morphed into a kind of homestead speakeasy, with days and nights of food, music, and midnight fire-pits. Gastronauts convened at long tables set with big white plates, bursting peonies in mason jars and, all around, an electric rainbow of lacquered steel Fermob chairs, each a different shock of color against the sky. The bathroom is in the "tiny house," a microcosm of this new breed of farm life: barn-wood walls, books galore, a sleekly modern slipper bathtub, and bunk beds for the kids.

Meanwhile, Wild Goose hatched another idea, a monthly showcase for a growing underground of cooks and newcomers not attached to traditional restaurants. On that cool "June-uary" afternoon, Wild Goose introduced newcomer-chef Thomas Boyce, fresh from the trenches of Wolfgang Puck's high-flying Spago Beverly Hills. Boyce and his star-baker wife, Kim, embody the migration of culinary talent bailing from cosmopolitan centers to mine Portland's "anything goes" attitude. The menu captured what he might bring to the local table: elegant oysters beneath finely grated radishes; a ravishing spring salad, with each vegetable cut to reveal hidden beauty; and wood oven–roasted salmon with skin as crispy as bacon. For dessert, hand-folded, cornmeal-crusted rhubarb tartlettes as round as their maker, an eight-months-pregnant Kim Boyce.

Two days later, the word buzzed through the blogo-sphere as Boyce was tagged to transform Portland's swanki-est food perch, Bluehour. Doulis received news, too, but nothing to celebrate: a phone call from zoning enforcement. "We received a complaint," said the man on the horn, issuing a warning. That's how it works on Sauvie Island. Black-tailed deer and sandhill cranes are not the only animals out here. Watchdogs live on the island, too, and they're not from the petting zoo at the pumpkin patch.

According to the *Portland Tribune* newspaper, unsigned letters circulated in 2009 encouraging islanders "to report to county planning officials" any activities out of step with Sauvie Island's exclusive farm-use zoning ordinances. In money-strapped Multnomah County, the complaint

system alone drives official "visits" and investigations. "Unfortunately," said one commissioner, "it's the financial reality we live in."

Now Doulis is wading through land-use documents and navigating the slalom course of Oregon's farmland protection laws that don't want crops replaced with cafés. He even asked a county inspector to walk through his property. "It's like vampires," he says with a heavy heart. "You have to invite them in."

Red tape has never been the province of the experimental food scene. But Doulis is working furiously on a compliance plan. "It's a lot of stuff for a couple of frickin' dinners. All last week, great cherries were coming in. But mostly, I'm eating up time on lawyers."

Coop de Grace

Portland is having a chicken moment. On an episode of *Portlandia* called "Is It Local?," a mythical chicken dish comes to stand for a restaurant culture gone slightly insane, as a waitress offers two suspicious diners a reassuring dossier on the bird in question, complete with photo ID, dietary habits, and a name, Colin. It's the most talked about spoof on the cult television show.

But even before *Portlandia* aired in 2011, Portland had bred a community with online chicken chat rooms, a hen-sitter business, and a Backyard Poultry Meetup Group whose motto is "We're eggcited to have you visit with us." In Portland, America's urban backyard-hen headquarters, residents can keep up to three chickens (or pygmy goats) without a permit. Even Mayor Sam Adams keeps a brood, all named Alma.

Chicken coops are serious business here, getting the same design attention as a hand-knit sweater. Some look like modernist homes, with heated floors and elaborate millwork, and many espouse green philosophies, eco roofs, and compost bins. The feeding frenzy is on full display at the annual Tour de Coops, a self-guided stroll through Portland's eastside hen 'hood. Raffle tickets are sold in a nearby church parking lot, where the roving Burgerville bus flips cage-free egg sandwiches.

Yianni Doulis has chickens, too. They're the pride of the Wild Goose Farm dinners, tucked into chunky chicken terrines or roasted to auburn perfection in the wood oven. But first Doulis has to kill them. His meat birds, bred for the table, are not poultry stars with Hollywood names. Doulis calls them stupid and aggressive, vacant as plants. Unlike his laying hens, he feels no connection to them.

Still, taking a life is a serious thing. He could have headed for the processing plant. Instead, he enrolled in "Kill Your Own Chicken" classes. The point was to stare them in the face. When the day arrived, he did just that. "It was like crossing a plateau, a profound day," he recalls. "It left me feeling crappy and thoughtful. I did it again this year. They tasted really good."

Doulis's birds had their first close-up in 2010 at a late-summer feast showcasing Timothy Bartling, inspired by his years at San Francisco's Zuni Café, home of the famed wood oven–roasted chicken. A recent transplant to Portland, Bartling lives for extreme rustic cooking. As a lodge cook in the Alaskan bush, he grilled caribou and moose in the far-flung wilderness, sometimes choppering guests to mountaintops for curated picnics of wild berries and king crab. At a sheep farm in Italy, he roasted suckling pigs in a fifteenth-century brick oven. Which is why he didn't flinch when, fifteen minutes before dozens of curious eaters were scheduled to arrive for the Sauvie Island dinner, three

combines at a neighboring farm revved up their engines, engulfing Wild Goose in a doomsday dust cloud, raining sandy ash on the lovingly set tables.

Doulis called and begged his neighbors to wait for another day. Nope. He tried another strategy: sending his kids over crying. Came back the word: Nope.

Bartling carried on valiantly, running a marathon between the barn kitchen and the outdoor oven, pulling out beautifully baked ricotta over thick-cut tomatoes, fat birds imprinted with char and smoke, and giant rounds of free-form plum *crostatas*, each a definitive denouement.

"I wanted everything to come out of this new oven Yianni was so proud of," recalls Bartling. "This kind of cooking is not for everyone. The clock is ticking. Bees are chasing you around. You're sweating your ass off, trying to make it look graceful without the comfort of a regular kitchen. I love the challenge. Things happen. It could have been a thunderstorm. You let it go, and let it happen. Everyone had dust in their nostrils, but it all worked out."

Parting Thoughts

Uncertainty about the future of the Wild Goose dinners and how to make a living has left Doulis feeling a bit twitchy and sleep deprived. But one thing gives him hope: the positive response. "I feel we touched a nerve, a pent-up need for these kinds of communal dinners," he says. "People are looking to get close to food." Maybe Wild Goose dinners let us dream a little ourselves, about what life might be like if we, too, threw away everything familiar and gambled on the serenity and challenges of farm life, away from the city.

For now, the goal is to grow things and grow community. Given the one-event-per-quarter rule Oregon imposes on farmland zones, Wild Goose is eyeing fall for its next dinner. Doulis sounds resolved to accept whatever fate brings. "Maybe we evolve into something else, a club, where friends gather. We don't talk about money, ever. There's a jar. I just butchered my chickens. Come eat them. It's a party. We like doing that anyway."

WILD GOOSE FROMAGE BLANC

Fromage blanc was the gateway cheese that led Yianni Doulis to an abiding passion, and his creamy soft cheese (think chèvre, or cream cheese without the guilt) is a fixture at his farm table alongside wood-roasted fruit. Easy to master, it requires only a few steps (over three days), a few specifics, and lots of caution. Sterilize all equipment and countertops. Use a "mesophilic" bacterial starter culture (MA 4001/4002 is his favorite), and raw milk, if you can find it. Everything else can be improvised or found at a cheese supply store. Stainless-steel teapot strainers from an Asian supermarket make great molds. For equipment and tips, visit Dairy Connection (DairyConnection.com) or Oregon's own Kookoolan Farms (www.kookoolanfarms.com).

1 gl/3.75 L whole cow or goat milk (not "flash" or UHT pasteurized), ideally raw

$1/8$ tsp freeze-dried mesophilic starter culture

5 drops veal rennet, or $1/4$ rennet tablet

Fine sea salt or fleur de sel

Paprika or fresh chopped herbs (optional)

1. Pour the milk into a stainless-steel pot, leaving at least 2 in/5 cm head room. Place the pot in a sink filled with hot (100°F/38°C) tap water, making sure the water doesn't go over the top of the pot and checking the temperature with an accurate thermometer. Stir the milk to distribute the heat. Once the milk reaches 80°F/28°C, immediately remove the pot from the sink. Sprinkle the starter culture over the surface, and then gently stir the milk without making bubbles.

2. Cover the pot and leave it in a warm place (near the stove or in the attic, for example), about 72°F/25°C, to ripen for 12 to 24 hours. The longer it ripens, the more acidic the final flavor.

3. Add the rennet, one drop at a time, stirring very gently just to combine. Cover and return the pot to the warm place for another 12 to 24 hours. When the cheese resembles yogurt and a layer of whey forms on the surface, it's ready. The curd may begin to separate from the sides of the pot.

4. Line sterile cheese molds with damp sterile cheesecloth. With a small spoon, gently scoop the curds into the molds, trying not to break up the curd mass. (The more you jostle it, the less the recipe will yield.) Set the molds on a draining rack and return them to a warm place. Cover with a large blanket of sterile cheesecloth and let drain for 24 to 48 hours.

5. Carefully remove the molds from the draining rack and place on a cheesecloth-lined baking sheet or platter. Dry the draining rack and line it with two layers of cheesecloth. One at a time, pick up the molds and turn over carefully to remove the cheese, catching it in one hand. (Discard the cheesecloth that lined the molds.) With the other hand, sprinkle a fine layer of sea salt over the surface of the cheese and place it upside down on the draining rack. Let the salt dissolve for at least 2 hours, at room temperature. Finish with a dash of paprika (if using). Refrigerate, covered, for up to 2 weeks.

MAKES ABOUT 1 LB/455 KG

BALSAMIC-ROASTED CHERRIES

The Mighty's own Teri Gelber battled grill flames, Bunsen burners, and summer heat to kick off Wild Goose Farm's first underground dinner, showing off her seasonal know-how, elegant simplicity, and deep roots in California's food scene. These easy roasted cherries are seasonal stunners with their sweet-tart caramelized juices and long stems—the perfect sidekick to duck and pork or, as a dinner closer, alongside *fromage blanc* or ice cream.

1 lb/455 kg fresh unpitted sweet cherries, with stems

2½ tsp extra-virgin olive oil

¼ cup/60 ml aged balsamic vinegar

¼ tsp fleur de sel

1 sprig fresh rosemary

1 sprig fresh thyme

1. Preheat the oven to 400°F/200°C/gas 6 or prepare a wood-burning oven until hot.

2. Place the cherries in a medium glass or ceramic baking dish. Stir in the olive oil, vinegar, and salt. Pull a few leaves off the sprigs of rosemary and thyme and toss them (sprigs and leaves) into the cherries. Stand the cherries upright so that the stems are pointing up, packing them closely together. Cover the dish with aluminum foil, and roast until the juices are released, about 15 minutes.

3. Remove the foil (carefully avoiding the released steam) and return the pan to the oven to roast the cherries until caramelized, about 5 minutes. Serve warm or at room temperature.

SERVES 8

CHAPTER 5

FOOD-CART REBELS

Portland's pavement gourmets create food malls and town squares of the future.

To make his masterpiece BLT, local winemaker and foodie-cum-eccentric, John Dovydenas, snags a sourdough loaf from a Moffat oven tucked inside his mobile food "cabin" and whacks off a couple of yeasty slabs. Each slice of bread is a canvas for an obsessive culinary vision that catapults the iconic sandwich into the pantheon of "must-eats." The bacon hails from a brined Portland pig, soaked for five days in honey and black pepper, and then hyper-smoked for six hours in a metal box hidden behind his handmade shed. The belly of the beast is roasted inside the cart, then trimmed into thick strips imbued with the flavor of damp bark, his secret fuel, which emits the smell of the Oregon backwoods and the taste of good whiskey. Next, come thick heirloom tomatoes and faintly bitter red oak lettuce, scored from the Wealth Underground Farm, a wilderness vegetable patch tended to by three twenty-somethings and, as it happens, the scene of the fictional hippie farm in the spoof hit *Portlandia.*

This pork-focused culinary magic is performed in a place called Picnic, a whimsical name for a food cart parked on a tawdry patch of asphalt in the city's nerve center. The petite structure, opened in spring 2011, has oak slat floors, barn wood siding, handsome cabinetry, and a pitched attic, all beautifully joined without a single nail. Over two years, Dovydenas built every inch, imagining a restaurant-caliber laboratory for his baking and sandwich experiments with the comforts of home. For a welcome mat, he paved the sidewalk out front with bricks. His refrigerator hosts ongoing sprout projects, the stove throws gas flames, and the bread oven, complete with steam injector and proofer chamber, greets two daily varieties to bracket fresh-smoked ham or local goat cheese paired with an entire lawn of cart-grown wheatgrass. It's luxurious by Portland food-cart standards, where a cobble-together, necessity-is-the-mother-of-invention mentality rules, but shows how far the genre can go.

Nearby, sidewalk connoisseurs can savor Japanese ramen, habit-forming deep-fried Mars bars, Cuban *batidos*, seared foie gras and chips, and healthful rice-and-bean bowls notched up by a "secret" garlic sauce that makes followers see chakra colors. Down the block at The People's Pig, even the egg salad gets a wallop of pork aïoli. Visiting Microsoft honcho Mike Angiulo summed up his

experience in one giddy snort: "It was pork and more pork on top of pork products—all topped with porky excellence." Porklandia par excellence.

Welcome to the feast streets of Portland, Oregon, headquarters for America's maverick food-cart movement. Not every option is ambitious, and a good number fail to rise above mediocre, but no gastropolis puts it together like Portland's pavement gourmets. The sheer volume of experimenters, the artisanal spirit, the punk-rock attitude, and, not least, minimal red tape and friendly licensing fees have galvanized these seminomadic kitchen tribes. Most cart owners around the country go it alone, fighting entrenched vendors for turf like drug lords in *The Wire*, or driving food trucks to ever-shifting locations to duck stiff fines and labyrinthian parking regulations.

Portland has thrived with a new urban cart model: dedicated spaces or "pods" where rent-paying carts coalesce to foster communal dining. Roughly twenty-five lots now house the majority of the city's 600-plus food carts, and the number is growing. This is where free-thinking vendors cook alongside old-schoolers in idiosyncratic, bike-friendly shacks, expressing Portland's bootstrapping brand of DIY capitalism.

Each pod is an outgrowth of its neighborhood, reflecting the cultural bent of its inhabitants, who gather in these outdoor food malls to eat, socialize, and dream up ideas for even more food carts. Some proprietors hang names at the pod's entrance; utopian titles that sound like parodies of Portland are especially popular. Cartopia, on busy Southeast Twelfth and Hawthorne Boulevard, a bridge hop from downtown, feels like an all-night gypsy food camp. According to some observers, it inspired the pod revolution in 2009, as citizens of the night flocked to a scene of anarchist crêpe makers and fry cooks. North Portland's Mississippi Marketplace is the opposite: financed and landscaped, with ten spiffy wagons, a Slow Food mentality, and customized water and power grids; it's Rodeo Drive by jerry-rigged cart standards. Mississippi's secret weapon is The Big Egg, a street-side temple to fried-egg sandwiches, each a model of perfection and worth the twenty-five-minute wait.

Portland's cart-o-mania seems irrepressible. Good Food Here is a boisterous mash-up of stalls and trucks

with a centralized mess hall enclosed by what looks like plastic shower curtains. Cartlandia touts itself as Portland's first "bike-centric food-cart super pod." D-Street Noshery captures the whimsy of modern "cartitecture," with each cart boasting a different design, twinkling in the night as a torch throws flames the height of a small child. Meanwhile, pop-up pods germinate in odd cracks and graffiti-slathered corners along Northeast Alberta Street, where neighborhood families relax alongside exiles in thought, manner, and gastronomy.

Picnic lives in a pod with no name: the culinary shantytowns of downtown Portland, where colorfully ramshackle carts hug the perimeters of parking lots, a short walk from prime hotels. Similar cart cities are spot-welded just a few blocks away. These bustling international cart districts dispense a global stew of Hungarian goulash, Mexican *sopes*, and hand-stretched Chinese noodles. One place promises "anything you can stuff in a dumpling." For businessmen, minivan moms, and tourists, these are the "gateway pods."

Each pod is a reimagined town square. To many, they are modern-day, Occupy Wall Street–leaning, preapocalyptic versions of Main Street, circa 2012, where the drugstore soda fountains, lunch diners, and bakeries that lined American towns during the quiet, narcotized Eisenhower years have now been replaced by street-ready dining houses on wheels. The mood is encapsulated downtown every day at noon, when duck confit sandwiches slide through the window at Addy's Sandwich Bar moments after trays of salt-cured, slow-cooked bird legs ride out of a demented oven beneath a cockeyed chandelier. When Addy Bittner, in her black high-top sneaks and camouflage tee, layers the earthy meat with her delicate apricot sauce and fresh pickled onions, you enter a world preoccupied by nuance. The moment sharpens as Public Enemy shouts *Fight the Power* from the kitchen's boom box.

Portland has long hosted an ethnic-based food-cart tradition fueled by immigrants in search of solid footing in the free market emporium known as America. But a new stratum in alfresco dining is evolving to another level as garage gourmets remake street food in their own image, to their own liking. According to *Eat Street*, a Cooking Channel show about street food, Portland vies for the

highest concentrations of food carts on the continent. Visitors who once made a beeline for Oregon's great outdoors, now arrive at the airport and say, "Take me to the food carts." New cart births and deaths are tracked on the blog FoodCartsPortland.com, which promotes the scene with the fervor of Don King. Even the local tourist bureau has hitched a ride.

Despite unprecedented growth, the cart owners' fiercest competitor is the weather. During winter's gloom, many carts go offline, and pods that jump like street parties in sunnier days look postapocalyptic. Can a place called Picnic survive the soggy chill that threatens these outdoor food emporia as winter rolls in? John Dovydenas has divined the answer. Eight months after opening, Picnic will shutter for the season while Dovydenas focuses on a winery housed in his Southeast Portland basement. Instead of discouragement, he's already dreaming up spring's menu: cart-fresh bagels to pair with line-caught salmon procured "from a friend of a friend of a friend who has a boat." The call of this new cart world is personal. He's curating his world, his way, and for now that's enough.

Cartopia: Birth of the Rock-'n'-Roll Pod

On a snowy night in 2009, the white plastic tent finally caved. For hours, the flimsy sheet struggled valiantly to protect a twisted picnic table, a cluster of tree-trunk stools, and the evening's host, cart owner Mike McKinnon, the chief decorator, dishwasher, and french fry fanatic behind the Potato Champion. This late-night nosh pit, parked on a half-empty lot in Southeast Portland, resonated with the underground music community, where McKinnon connected as a drummer. Gregg Abbott, a sometime musician and professional slacker, was also out in the cold. He drifted up to the window for a midnight *poutine*, a Canadian comfort heap of fries, brown gravy, and cheese curds—and a remarkable feast in a neighborhood where good food goes to bed at ten p.m.

McKinnon invited Abbott to warm up inside, and conversation rolled. Abbott, just the wrong side of thirty, was tired of parking cars for a living at a steakhouse. The social pressures were coming at him, even in "anything goes" Portland. For days, he kept asking himself, "What can I do in the next ninety days to be more than I am?"

Looking around McKinnon's cart, he found the answer. "I saw a community piling around this place. Mike wasn't just one of those guys who stands around doing nothing. He was building something. I felt empowered."

The next day he called his chef dad for advice and opened a Twitter account to spread the word. His making-of-a-cart communiqués caught the ear of bloggers and a growing vegan-tech crowd. Three months later, only twenty-five paces from the Potato Champion, Whiffies Fried Pies opened with Abbott's smart-phone army at the window. Even before the first bite of peanut butter cream and chocolate chips oozed from a hot pocket of golden dough, Whiffies had the whiff of a cult hit.

The lure of food trucks seemed irresistible to Portlanders looking for a way to re-enter the American Dream machine. For over a year, from his bedroom vantage point behind the parking lot, construction worker Dustin Knox watched carts come and topple, including the milkshake shack that missed the memo on Portland's ten-month sweater season. But one place caught his attention: Potato Champion, a rocking house of Belgian *frites* holding vigil until three a.m., and drawing ecstatic club kids. "It was the middle of January. The rain was coming sideways at one A.M., and orders for potatoes doubled. I knew I had to open a food cart."

Knox's food-world dossier: a dishwashing job at IHOP. No matter. He had a vision: a theatrical crêpe cart with crazy combos folded like obsessive laundry into large-format, paper-wrapped packets right before your eyes. He found a relic food wagon at a fairground in Seattle and remodeled it with copper-lined details. Three weeks later, he pulled up his shiny white vehicle next to Potato Champion, filled it with music and gauzy light, and gave it a fancy name, Perierra Crêperie. From the open storefront-size window, steam from humongous cast-iron griddles rose like a fog machine; the Notorious B.I.G. rapped so emphatically, the wagon swayed like a hula dancer.

By late April 2009, with dance parties erupting and the blogosphere buzzing, Cartopia, America's first rock 'n' roll food cart corral was up and positively running. In May, the *New York Times* showed up. In his "Frugal Portland" piece, writer Matt Gross salivated over the city's affordable gastronomy and budding street-food scene. "As a New Yorker, I was jealous . . . overjoyed at what I could find within a single pod." After that, all hell broke loose. Lines formed before the windows opened. Every night was a party.

"It was a youthful, let's put it out there, nothing can stop us moment," recalls Knox. Cars and customers jostled for supremacy. One night, a dozen women arrived with their own idea: a fold-out table, linen, and candles. With food curated from six carts, they popped open Champagne and staged a guerrilla dinner party right then, right there. Knox was struck like Moses at the burning bush. The cars had to go. He built a dozen picnic tables, then laid them out with an invitation to dine communally at the country's new food-cart table.

The response was swift. On July 4, nearly 1,000 eaters showed up in the city's new living room. With Ghostface Killah's boom baps in the backdrop, food spilled out of cart windows to a swirl of humanity—black kids and goth girls, drunken frat boys, gay couples, a few seniors, a busload of teachers, and a preacher and his son, all eating together, finding friendship and food salvation in a revival tent atmosphere. Even the police came . . . to eat.

Far from megachains, three outcast impresarios reimagined the meeting ground and culinary ethos of *Fast Food Nation*: an open-air food court and impromptu dance hall feeding the zeitgeist for something cheap, wonderful, and handmade. McKinnon, Abbott, and Knox changed our perspective of what an outdoor space could be. Nothing quite like it existed anywhere, not in the food-cart worlds of New York, Bangkok, or even downtown Portland, where dedicated food-cart alleys, however interesting, lacked seating and a shared vision.

Thirty-five days after opening, Abbott was a cover boy in *The Mercury*, a local alternative weekly. Calls came fast and furiously from journalists, cart hopefuls, and curious city officials from around the country; Knox delisted his phone number. Everyone who saw the place was equally shocked and smitten. Tourists swelled, the Food Channel knocked, and camera crews became as familiar as take-out boxes. Within a year, Portland's cart-housing project spread to other neighborhoods, revitalizing forgotten concrete and dirt plots with urban life and budding entrepreneurial dreams.

"Nationally, we made something happen," says Knox. "People craved an outdoor space that wasn't corporatized. That image of hundreds of people of all stripes hanging out, talking and eating, wandering around a parking lot strung with lights. It hit on something pop culture didn't allow. It put ripples through the country."

The Sugar Cube: The Sweet and the Bitter

In 2008, The Sugar Cube shot out of nowhere with conceptual Betty Crocker cupcakes and "triple-chocolate-threat" cookies containing a lifetime of pleasure. Spice cakes reborn with Guinness stout and mousselike maple cream cheese frosting vaulted from Kir Jensen's snow-white trailer in downtown Portland. Made from her own wild-child cake mixes, these confections sent early smoke signals from Portland's budding food-cart blocks. The Amy Winehouse Cupcakes said it all: a crown of chocolate frosting as elegant as Audrey Hepburn garnished with a brazen "coke" straw and a pile of powdered sugar. A new day in baking, indeed.

Followers circled regularly, ready to raid the daily inventory from an oven tended by a tattooed redhead wearing her hearts on her sleeve—literally. Word of the latest Sugar Cube find spread like a hot stock tip. But customers often found more than heavenly treats; Jensen had the look of a woman on the verge, tearfully running her first business without a financial plan or viable equipment. Six months after opening, and just weeks after national notice in *Sunset* magazine, Jensen folded, cash strapped and fried by one too many electrical shorts.

The Sugar Cube resurfaced again in November 2009. Jensen, older and cart-wiser, pulled into the Mississippi Marketplace in North Portland with a security blanket microloan, an upgraded trailer, and a new definition of what her cart could be: a dessert bar serving haute treats on a budget. Sugar Cube became a revolutionary experiment in "sweetgeist," an unstoppable parade of miraculous, hand-hewn munchies that reinvented the sweet zone; caramel sauce as smoky as bacon, chocolate cupcakes impaled with potato chips, apple crisp coiffed in a dust of fennel pollen, and other revisions of the familiar. Taste buds and critical praise soared. A month later, the pipes froze, icicles gripped the faucet, and Jensen skated across the

trailer floor. Suffice it to say, the butter did not reach room temperature. The Sugar Cube shut its oven door again.

For all the romance and media love, feast street is not easy street. Cart owners are under constant stress, confronting power outages, financial uncertainty, limited space, and physical discomfort. Jensen doesn't have the room to store a forty-pound bag of sugar like most pastry chefs, and shopping runs are a matter of survival: the farmers' market, the artisan salt shop, the chocolate guys, the local whiskey house, the grocery store staples. She calls every day a struggle: "I'm a solo operator. I'm lugging around ten-pound bags. I'm the garbage lady. You can't just clock in and clock out. I don't have fifteen assistants. In the winter, it's cold; in the summer, turning on the oven is an act of insanity."

So what is the lure? In exchange for logistical challenges, cart owners get to test-drive ideas, call the shots, creative and otherwise, with the chance to build a name—or maybe an empire—without digging themselves into an unsightly financial hole. Opening a new restaurant in Portland costs $100,000 to $250,000; a new bakery might require $500,000. But cart owners are not beholden to big banks, private equity, or investor syndicates. ROI means *return on inventiveness*. Curbside entrepreneurs can get in the game for around $30,000, more or less.

Jensen's cooking path started in a Chicago culinary school. She left one class short of a degree, noting, "I hate fondant." Wearing a toque in an Evanston kitchen while baking elaborate desserts she didn't believe in became meaningless. She knew what she liked, "Simple. Not twenty elements. Not just ingredients on a plate that looks crazy and conceptual. Five flavors, that's it, all harmonious."

When she bought her first cart in downtown, Jensen could only afford a beaten-down trailer littered with used drug needles and smelling of a barn. For months she painted, scrubbed, and imagined a path to making her own decisions. "It was tiny as hell, but it was beautiful. I wasn't meant to take orders from anyone else. I've crawled my way to do what I do."

The Sugar Cube has yet another new home, the Good Food Here pod on Southeast Belmont, where piercings and hemp clothes are as familiar as old Victorians. In this brave new world, ambitious vegans ply earth-friendly

dreams alongside purveyors of over-the-top meat sloth. You can find escargot in a paper cup and maple ice cream flavored with "humanely raised and hormone-free bacon." A shiny red fold-out diner pulses with tempeh Reubens and jah love, day and night, and a place called Lardo sells gut-stretching sandwiches informed by in-cart butchery and homemade mustard. At the entrance, an ATM stands ready to feed you money.

The Sugar Cube occupies the northern west end, where Jensen whips up new refreshments daily. This summer belonged to Banana What What Shakes sporting candied maple bacon swizzle sticks and gingersnap ice cream sandwiches bound in the wild crunch of sesame brittle. Three years into this food-cart journey, her walls are lined with accolades from local and national press. *Saveur* magazine was recently in the house, eating through the menu. StarChefs.com, the Who's Who of the restaurant world, named Jensen a "rising pastry star 2011"—a rarity for a cart owner. She even got a book deal: *The Sugar Cube: 50 Deliciously Twisted Treats from the Sweetest Little Food Cart on the Planet* arrived last year. Will she be open next time you drive by? Who can say? But on any given day, a food cart on Southeast Belmont is whipping up the most inspired treats in town.

Yet, Jensen ekes out little more than thirty dollars on some days. One day she's killing it, the next, everything fades to black. Meanwhile, the price of top-notch ingredients doesn't change. To Jensen, the customer phrase "You want *six dollars* for that?" is nothing less than a stake through the heart. "I want to say to them, 'Go to Safeway and get that cake that weighs three pounds,'" she wails one afternoon. She eyes the brick-and-mortar life with a bit of envy—the normal plumbing, the heating, the air conditioning, the alcoholic beverages—an instant source of profit. She can't understand why restaurants are battling the carts. "The grass is always greener," she sighs. "I don't point fingers. I don't just sit back and 'whaa whaa.' Everybody's busting ass. The cart has done wonderful things for me. But this is not a get-rich scheme. It's do or die all the time."

My Vision, My Values, My Baby

Philadelphia salesman Kevin Bell was twenty-six when he read a magazine article about Portland—the mystique, the

Most Frequently Asked Questions at the Sugar Cube

Is it good?

Is it vegan?

Is it gluten-free?

Is it sugar-free?

mountains, the offbeat culture, and, not least, the great coffee. Intrigued, he paid a visit in 2009 and remembers seeing green everywhere, shades of lush that scrambled his brain. The air was clean and smelled of possibility. In Philly, he was doomed to be that same guy forever; in Portland, he could be anybody or somebody. The deal was cinched halfway through a meal at the Potato Champion. Here was something young, fun, and smart, making money *and* making people happy. Far from Philly's roach coaches and hot-dog vendors, the culture and cuisine of Portland's food carts resonated, and so did a city of haunting beauty and soulful gloom. "Sometimes everything crystalizes in near-death moments, or when you fall in love," says Bell. "That moment for me was eating *poutine* in the rain at Potato Champion." He rented an apartment the next day.

In his new persona, Bell peddles Italian ice water, a frozen sorbetlike treat and a favorite on Philly's mean streets and Jersey's shores. But gone are the corn syrups, lurid colors, and carnival flavors of his youth. Extreme localism stands at the center of his Oregon Ice Works, a silver cargo trailer parked in the D-Street Noshery pod. Bell is now a man unbound, attacking life, obsessed with peak seasons and the science of mouthfeel, the ability to extrude creamy illusions from fruit, water, and organic cane sugar. Bell plays it cool and super-natural. His marionberry batches celebrate the integrity of gritty seeds; peach clings to skins; and pear ice exudes an authentic grainy pitch. The intensity pays off; these scoops are pure, ingenious joy. Bell samples each harvest like a DJ, collaging seasons, pluck, and purpose into an essential expression of food-cart life in a food-centric city. "I'm not going to sell just anything for a buck," he says. "This is my chance. My vision, my values, my baby."

Whatever the hardships, start-up dreamers keep crashing this culinary frontier. Bell heralds a second wave of Portland's maverick cart owners looking to escape the nine-to-five punch-clock world where the corporate overlords micromanage every move. The new guard includes Captured by Porches Guerrilla Public House, where four kinds of craft beers flow into mason jars. The brew cascades from outdoor taps protruding from a rusted, military green, red-hubcapped 1930s-era bread truck that conjures a ride from Castro's victory parade. The Hospitality Suite, a temporary craft cocktail wagon, shakes up local spirits, offers bartender tips, and tests the limits of local liquor laws.

With growth has come fears of a food-cart bubble. Rents are rising. Winters are unnerving, even for a motivated guy like Bell, who hopes Portlanders will plop down $100 to join his Oregon Ice Club, a weekly rotation of exclusive pints, one of several strategies in his survival kit. Is cart life viable? And for how long? Or will the movement evolve into something else?

Those were the questions whispered around pod towns when cart star Kevin Sandri upped and walked away from a scene he helped thrust into the national spotlight, abruptly closing his beloved Garden State in late 2011. Sandri was one of the first to cook like a top chef on a cart-owner's budget, connecting his East Coast Sicilian-American roots with Oregon's small-scale sodbusters who quietly fed his philosophy of sustainable eating with fresh-from-the-ground lettuce and biodynamic chickens. To lay down a tone-perfect Jersey meatball sandwich, he bargained for scraps of twenty-one-day aged beef. Imagine Tony Soprano heading the farm-to-table movement. That was Garden State. "I'm not running an elephant ear cart," said Sandri weeks after opening. "A food cart allows us to serve really good fast food at a reasonable price. It would be too bad if an expensive atmosphere is the only place to find great ingredients. We're bringing it to the people."

For four years, Garden State ruled Portland's food-cart chart. And then it was over. Poof. "The hilly-billy nature catches up with you. It's kind of like camping every day. I don't want to camp anymore."

Despite critical acclaim and what he terms "a good living," Sandri burned out on running a solo business. The hours, the headaches, the three break-ins . . . "and they always took the meatballs." While low overhead allowed him to invest in quality ingredients, 35 percent food costs—high, even by nice restaurant standards—left little margin for staff support. "You pull the burden yourself; that's the margin," Sandri points out. "Food carts are like eating a meal crafted in someone's home. It's a party at the core—that's what you're throwing. It's too personal, too direct to farm it out. Someone else doing Neil Young doesn't work."

Portland's quiet Sellwood neighborhood lucked out when Sandri's old-time string band went bust in 2007, and he decided to mine his love of cooking with a custom-built cart and a $30,000 loan. It was just a vacant spot on a quaint street; no one had heard of pods. Garden State was just an end run around the expense of opening a restaurant. Sandri had no inkling of the craze to come. "It went nuts, and I got to be part of it. *Good Morning America*, the Cooking Channel, hanging around my cart. It's been one hell of a run."

Over in Cartopia, Gregg Abbott is hunkering down for the winter, a week after *US News & World Report* ranked Portland the world's No. 1 street food scene, its gastronomic reach and utter friendliness vaulting over Singapore's hawker centers and Istanbul's teeming alfresco bazaars. On this brisk October evening, he's pulling fresh ideas from the fryer. Pumpkin turnovers bob in hot oil alongside golden crescents plumped with apples and bacon jam. What doesn't fly out of Wiffie's window will be donated as "OccuPIES" to the Wall Street protesters gathered downtown.

Abbott jumped into this adventure looking for hope and redemption. Early on, to meet demands, he rented a commissary kitchen. Since he was already running at capacity, the investment merely increased his sanity, not his wallet size. Last winter, he paid bills out of savings.

This year, Wiffies finally turned a profit. What if he had continued parking cars at the Ringside Steakhouse? Does he make more money now? Not really, says Abbott. Yet he is a richer man indeed. "I drive the same '96 Ford Explorer and live in the same apartment. But I'm involved in this super-cool thing. I get to feel creative, be part of a community. I'm a nerd who's into food. I can hang out with other nerds who are fanatic about food. Bunk's Tommy Habetz comes over to my place. He knows my name. People say, 'I know that guy.' Some nights standing at work, I can't believe this is happening . . . this huge sea of people. I finally did something that impacts people's lives."

THE BIG EGG'S ARBOR LODGE FRIED-EGG SANDWICH

Every breakfast joint has fried-egg sandwiches, but this yolk-colored cart in North Portland puts them on the pedestal as its raison d'être, each one artfully constructed with the unexpected, from fresh organic jam to nasturtium blossoms. Cartmeisters Gail Buchanan and Elizabeth D. Morehead are more slow food than short order. Their Monte Cristo, on cardamom-flecked French toast, is a legend, but the Arbor Lodge is the sleeper: beds of grilled, thick-cut portobellos and slow-cooked balsamic onions provide a cozy berth for an over-easy egg, and the sheets of crisp, hot brioche are lacquered with roasted-garlic mayo.

Roasted Garlic—Thyme Mayo

2 tsp olive oil

2 sprigs fresh thyme, plus 1 tbsp chopped fresh thyme

1 garlic head, top sliced off

1 cup/240 ml good-quality mayonnaise

1/8 tsp cayenne pepper

Kosher salt and freshly ground black pepper

Balsamic Onions

2 tsp unsalted butter

1/2 tsp olive oil

1 medium yellow onion, cut into 1/4-in-/6-mm-thick slices

Kosher salt

2 tsp aged balsamic vinegar

Mushrooms

5 tbsp/75 ml olive oil

1 large or 2 small portobello mushrooms, cut into 1/2-in-/12-mm-thick slices

Kosher salt and freshly ground black pepper

1 tbsp unsalted butter

2 eggs

4 thick slices brioche, buttered on one side

Kosher salt

2 handfuls of arugula

1. TO MAKE THE MAYO: Preheat the oven to 425°F/220°C/gas 7. Pour the olive oil onto a small area of a baking dish, and top with the thyme sprigs. Place the garlic head, cut-side down, over the herbs. Bake until the garlic is soft, 15 to 20 minutes. Cool, then squeeze about half the cloves into a bowl (eat the leftovers on bread). Mash with a spoon. Add the mayonnaise, chopped thyme, cayenne, and a good pinch of salt and pepper. Stir and mash until blended. Refrigerate until ready to use.

2. TO MAKE THE ONIONS: In a large skillet over medium-low heat, warm the butter and olive oil. Stir in the onion and a hefty pinch of salt. Cook until nicely caramelized, stirring occasionally, about 30 minutes. Stir in the vinegar, and remove from the heat.

3. TO SAUTÉ THE MUSHROOMS: In a large skillet over medium-high heat, heat 3 tbsp of the olive oil. Add the mushrooms, drizzle 1 tbsp olive oil on top, and season with a good pinch of salt and pepper. Cook until nicely browned, 4 to 5 minutes. Turn and drizzle with the remaining oil. Cook until lightly browned, caramelized around the edges, and soft to the touch but still firm, 2 to 3 minutes.

4. In a small skillet, heat the 1 tbsp butter over medium heat. Add the eggs and fry, turning once, until the edges are crisp but the yolk is still runny, about 2 minutes.

5. Meanwhile, heat a 12-in/30.5-cm nonstick sauté pan over medium-high heat. Spread 1 tsp of the mayonnaise over the unbuttered sides of each brioche slice. Grill the four slices, butter-side down, until golden brown. Remove the slices from the pan and, working quickly so the bread doesn't cool, crisscross the mushrooms over two slices (mayo-side up), then top each with caramelized onions (roughly 1 tbsp), a fried egg, a good pinch of salt, and a handful of arugula. Close the sandwiches with the remaining slices (mayo-side down) and serve immediately.

MAKES 2 SANDWICHES

THE SUGAR CUBE'S CHOCOLATE CARAMEL POTATO CHIP CUPCAKES

Portland food-cart iconoclast and baker extraordinaire Kir Jensen saved the cupcake genre from the clutches of boredom. From her inventive collection, these are the ultimate splurge: elegant chocolate buttermilk cakes, with big salty potato chips jutting wildly out of deep, dark chocolate ganache, all etched in Jensen's wicked caramel. Die now . . . with a smile.

Chocolate Buttermilk Cupcakes

3 cups/385 g unbleached all-purpose flour

2 ¾ cups/550 g sugar

1 cup/100 g Dutch-process cocoa powder

½ tsp kosher salt

1 tbsp plus 1½ tsp baking soda

1½ cups/360 ml buttermilk

1½ cups/360 ml strongly brewed or French-pressed coffee, cooled

3 eggs, at room temperature

1 tbsp pure vanilla extract

1⅓ cups/315 ml vegetable oil

Coffee Syrup

½ cup/120 ml strongly brewed coffee

½ cup/100 g sugar

1¼ cups/300 ml Kir's Salted Caramel Sauce, completely cooled (page 160)

1½ cups/360 ml Sexy Bittersweet Chocolate Ganache (page 161)

144 salted, ridged, whole potato chips, preferably Ruffles

1. TO MAKE THE CUPCAKES: Preheat the oven to 350°F/180°C/gas 4. Line 24 muffin cups with paper liners.

2. In a large bowl, sift together the flour, sugar, cocoa powder, salt, and baking soda. In a medium bowl, whisk together the buttermilk, coffee, eggs, vanilla, and vegetable oil. Whisk the wet ingredients into the dry ingredients, mixing just until incorporated and lump-free (it's a thin batter). Fill each muffin cup to within ¼ in/6 mm of the top. Bake until the tops spring back when gently pressed, 20 to 25 minutes, reversing the pans from front to back and top to bottom to ensure even baking after 15 minutes.

3. TO MAKE THE COFFEE SYRUP: Meanwhile, in a small saucepan over high heat, bring the coffee and sugar to a boil. Boil for 1 to 2 minutes to concentrate the mixture, then remove from the heat and brush the tops of the warm cupcakes with the coffee syrup. (You'll use most but not all of it. Save any leftovers for a cocktail.) Allow the cupcakes to cool completely before proceeding with the next step.

4. Pour the caramel sauce into a squeeze bottle or piping bag with narrow tip attached. Insert the tip into the top of the cupcakes and squeeze a little caramel into each one (they should plump up a bit, but don't overfill).

5. Dip the top of each cupcake in the cooled (but not cold; it must be thick and runny enough to coat the cupcakes) ganache, then tilt to remove the excess. Place on a large platter and let the chocolate set for about 30 minutes.

6. Drizzle a few streaks of the (room temperature) caramel sauce over the top, then impale the ganache with 6 potato chips. Drizzle more caramel sauce over the chips to serve.

MAKES 2 DOZEN

KIR'S SALTED CARAMEL SAUCE

Possibly the best caramel sauce you have ever eaten, with the lingering essence of smoke, brown butter, and salt, and just the right drizzle factor between thick and thin. Kir Jensen cooks it "to the razor's edge of deliciously deep and flat-out burnt" to tease out the complexity. Make it well in advance to assure the caramel is cool and thick enough to drizzle and fill the cupcakes.

2 cups/400 g sugar
1 cup/240 ml water
1½ tsp fleur de sel
2 cups/480 ml heavy cream, warm
1½ tsp pure vanilla extract

1. In a deep, heavy-bottomed pot, combine the sugar, water, and fleur de sel. Without stirring, cook over high heat until the sugar starts to color around the edges of the pot. Reduce the heat to medium-high and continue cooking, swirling the pan occasionally to help the caramel color evenly. Once the caramel is very dark mahogany in color and lightly smoking (on the verge of burning), immediately remove from the heat. Working quickly, add the cream in a steady stream (be careful; it will splatter), stirring the caramel with a wooden spoon. Cook over low heat for a few minutes to dissolve any lumps.

2. Strain through a fine-mesh sieve into a metal bowl. Stir in the vanilla, then cool at room temperature, stirring occasionally, for about 1½ hours. (Use for cupcakes at this stage.) Transfer to a glass jar and refrigerate up to 1 week. (If you make the caramel the day ahead, be sure to take it out of the refrigerator 4 to 6 hours beforehand, so it's soft enough to work with.)

MAKES ABOUT 2½ CUPS/600 ML

SEXY BITTERSWEET CHOCOLATE GANACHE

Kir Jensen doesn't skimp on butter in her chocolate ganache, which adds to the richness and sheen. Leftovers? Wake up and smell the chocolate ganache. Jensen spreads it on warm brioche with sea salt and olive oil to kickstart the day.

15 oz/430 g bittersweet chocolate, 64% cocoa or higher, roughly chopped
¾ cup plus 2 tbsp/200 g unsalted butter, cut into cubes
½ tsp fleur de sel
¼ cup/60 ml light corn syrup

In a medium stainless-steel bowl, combine the chocolate, butter, fleur de sel, and corn syrup. Place the bowl over a pan of barely simmering water and heat, stirring often, until the chocolate and butter have melted. Remove from the heat and let cool before using. Refrigerate up to 1 week.

MAKES ABOUT 3 CUPS/720 ML

THE SUGAR CUBE'S BANANA WHAT WHAT SHAKES

What's not to love about malted banana shakes stirred up in tall glasses with swizzle sticks of candied bacon draped in crunch, maple, and mustard? At the Sugar Cube cart, Kir Jensen keeps the flavor madness going with swirls of whiskey caramel sauce (made with some fine "white dog" from Portland's House Spirits distillery) and a cloud of "whoop" cream.

Whiskey Caramel Sauce

2 tbsp Kir's Salted Caramel Sauce (page 160)

2 tsp whiskey

Whoop

1/2 cup/120 ml heavy whipping cream, chilled

1 tbsp dark brown sugar

1/8 tsp pure vanilla extract

Shakes

1 large ripe banana, frozen and cut into chunks

2 to 3 scoops good-quality vanilla bean ice cream

1 heaping tbsp malt powder

1/2 to 3/4 cup/120 to 180 ml whole milk

2 slices Candied Maple Bacon for stir sticks (facing page)

1. TO MAKE THE WHISKEY CARAMEL SAUCE: Gently rewarm the caramel in a small saucepan over low heat for 1 to 2 minutes. Whisk the whiskey into the warm caramel and set aside.

2. TO MAKE THE "WHOOP": In a stand mixer fitted with the whisk attachment (or with a handheld mixer or simply by hand), whip the cream with the brown sugar and vanilla over medium-high speed until lightly whipped (not stiff).

3. TO MAKE THE SHAKE: In a blender, combine the banana, ice cream, malt powder, and enough milk to create the desired thickness. Blend on high speed until smooth and creamy, 1 to 2 minutes. Pour into two chilled 10-oz/300-ml glasses. Top each with a hefty dollop of whoop and a few ribbons of caramel sauce. Place one candied bacon slice in each glass and serve immediately.

MAKES TWO 10-OUNCE/300-ML SHAKES

THE SUGAR CUBE'S CANDIED MAPLE BACON

In Portland, only culinary monks and misfits flinch at candied bacon for breakfast. Kir Jensen goes a step further, adding sly notes of mustard and maple syrup to wake up jaded buds and then blasting away until the strips dance with halos of crunch and caramel. Jump-start the morning in style, or get in the Sugar Cube mode and pop a strip into a milkshake as a stir stick and a lick of piggy humor.

¼ cup/60 ml grade B maple syrup

¾ tsp Dijon mustard

2 grinds fresh black pepper

5 slices Nueske's or thick-cut applewood-smoked bacon

1. Preheat the oven to 400°F/200°C/gas 6. Line a baking sheet with parchment paper, and place a rack over the paper.

2. In a small bowl, combine the maple syrup, mustard, and pepper. Dip the bacon strips in the maple mixture to liberally coat both sides and arrange on the rack without overlapping. Bake until the edges start to crisp, about 10 minutes.

3. Remove the baking sheet from the oven, flip the strips, and baste with the remaining maple mixture. Bake until the bacon takes on a rich caramelized color and a lacquered sheen, about 10 minutes more, basting once more during the last 5 minutes. If you want to tear the bacon into pieces, let it cool completely first. Or you can cut each slice in half and serve.

MAKES 5 SLICES

CHAPTER 6

THE NEW PIONEERS

Small-batch coffee roasters, salumi fanatics, and daring entrepreneurs detour away from corporate models to blaze fresh trails.

ADAM McGOVERN & ARIC MILLER

COFFEEHOUSE NORTHWEST + STERLING COFFEE ROASTERS

Deep inside Portland's coffee revolution, two baristas take microroasting to the street.

Internet post, February 4, 2004:

We are excited to host the anti-Starbucks meeting tonight at the Infoshop, and look forward to sharing the new space with you all. As for what we will provide, we have a wide selection of tea available at the shop, but no coffee yet. We do have decaf coffee beans, but lack a grinder.

In Portland, even the Marxists have coffee standards.

The quality of the grind, the shade of the roast, the etch of the foam—it all matters here. To shortcut coffee is to not care, and to not care in Portland is akin to living in Detroit and advocating against cars. Blame it on—or credit— Stumptown Coffee Roasters. The hometown venture transformed black pools of liquid earth into an art form celebrating the downtrodden plantation farmer with the highest paid prices and fair practices. In this geeky world, coffee flavors arrive extruded and exalted in custom roasts, and lattes are served by tattooed baristas speaking in the vernacular of latter-day sommeliers.

For years, Stumptown, which borrowed Portland's goofy nickname, reigned over a city rebelling against Starbuck's expansionism and grande blandness. Stumptown's vinyl-spinning rock 'n' roll dripperies embodied Portland's food-first, do-it-yourself culture. But any coffee shop "trained" in Stumptown methodology was allowed to use the company's prized, single farm–grown beans. And between 2005 and 2008, to brandish the words "proudly serving Stumptown coffee"—often posted at local cash registers—was to be patriotic.

Then, in a slurp, things changed. A microroasting movement took hold, and the new cool was to not serve Stumptown. By 2011, within a downtown radius, no fewer than ten shops served their own point of brew, backed by an emerging think tank of microroasting nerds.

Courier Coffee exemplifies the new breed. Its leader, bike-riding roaster Joel Domreis, lives like a character in a graphic novel: in the shadows, cycling by dawn to deliver just-roasted beans to restaurants and individual addicts. Like everything at Courier, each bundle is tagged with handwritten notes. A turntable on the counter spins the house mood, Monk to Motley Crue; coffee is poured through 23-karat gold-plated filters into mason jars. Art exhibits come from regulars like Andy Warhol confidant Paige Powell,

whose rare, circa-1980s photographs of New York's downtown art stars turned heads on opening day. Asked Domreis, admiring the portraits, "Who is Basquiat?"

Over in Southeast Portland, the wired-in Coava Coffee Roasters, housed in the showroom of the Bamboo Revolution, obsesses over sustainability with its reusable "Kone," a laser-welded object of desire that combines the pour-over coffee fetish with French-press flavor. The first run of 1,000 sold out quickly at $50 a pop.

Blocks away, on emerging East Burnside, pro snowboard idol Wille Yli-Luoma heads his own school of thought at Heart Coffee Roasters. His vaguely Scandinavian roast, as light and pure as the driven snow, arrives in a Finnish science lab–cum-schoolhouse, as rock music soars and a black Probat roaster grinds away in the middle of the room. His geeky toy? A halogen-powered Hiakari siphon bar, one of a handful in the United States, costing more than your car. If you've ever thrilled to the sight of a death ray, the siphon bar is for you. It shoots out *Star Trek*–ian transporter light beams, pumps thermonuclear colors, whirls up raging bubbles, sucks coffee grounds dry, and then extracts every particle of flavor to produce a $6 cup just for you.

But even in this group, Coffeehouse Northwest and Sterling Coffee Roasters stand apart.

In 2005, Adam McGovern and Aric Miller wanted to be the best in Portland. Not the biggest or the hippest coffee shop but the guys who did it right. It would not be easy. Their Coffeehouse Northwest sits on a downtrodden stretch of West Burnside, a land of desperadoes, bad parking juju, and early construction nightmares across the street that made the place shake like a Disneyland shuttle-simulation ride.

Meanwhile, the coffee cognoscenti poured into the Albina Press, where rising star Billy Wilson, the pierced-tongue prince of latte art, held sway with Stumptown beans and a house arrogance that added to the house mystique. When Wilson dropped by one day, McGovern and Miller were petrified to serve him. For the next two years they competed in their minds against Albina, practicing techniques like wired-up Larry Birds, doing chin-ups in the back during breaks. It was the Mets vs. the Yankees, Rocky vs. Ivan. The Albina Press barely knew they existed. It didn't matter; behind the intensely focused McGovern, word spread:

The *macchiatos* were models of purity; the cappuccinos a religious experience; the espresso balanced like the scales of justice.

But Coffeehouse Northwest offered something more profound than the perfect drink: a grand sense of hospitality, a childlike embrace of holidays, and a profound love of music, generously traded between staff and customers. Something lost was found at Coffeehouse Northwest; to come here was to go home.

The spirit is best expressed every Thanksgiving when the staff, decked in vintage finery, works the holiday without pay, serving free drinks to the hordes all day long, then pooling tip money for charity. The night ends with a pop-up potluck dinner, the most inspired Thanksgiving spread ever presented in aluminum foil pans. As the invitation says: "Anyone totally welcome."

Even Billy Wilson felt the pull. In 2008, he took a job at Coffeehouse Northwest, soaking in the art of the friendly, then opened his acclaimed Barista nearby in the Pearl District.

The Poetry of the Street

In 2009, as Coffeehouse Northwest's stature grew, McGovern and Miller hatched a plan for expansion: Think small. They set up a secret R&D coffee-roasting lab in McGovern's bedroom, hanging a hose out of the window to disperse the fumes. Eight months later, for their second act, they threw away coffee-shop conventions at Sterling Coffee Roasters, taking roasting right to the street in an open-air structure decorated like a London bar. The feel is elegant, romantic, and witty, with a whiff of defiance—Cary Grant with a neck tattoo.

So what do two guys with dapper tastes pack into a minuscule coffee kiosk on a shoestring budget? Old books, candle-lit sconces, a porcelain pheasant, three stately Robur E coffee grinders, and a steampunk roaster that looks on loan from a railway museum. The ultimate splurge: hand-painted wallpaper from England's Farrow & Ball, a few meters of indulgence for $1,000. Next to a shiny Synesso espresso machine, brown lunch bags promise "Delicious Croissants"—only a dozen per day, the entire inventory from the renegade Broken Frame Bakery.

Then there's McGovern and Miller, working shoulder to shoulder in these snug quarters, bantering like characters in a buddy cop movie on subjects as far-flung as *Calvin and Hobbes*, James Joyce, and Joey Lawrence. Without missing a beat, they hawk-eye the roaster (one slip of distraction could spell disaster for the day's batch) and monitor weights and timers for exacting espresso pulls while acting as party hosts, making sure every customer is part of the conversation.

Sterling's young crew, tight-knit and impossibly affable, is always dressed to the hilt: wingtips, ascots, and tucked-in ties for the lads; pillbox hats and vintage bling for the ladies. Even in the winter, when the flames under the roaster constitute the house heater, style matters. When Sterling opened in February 2010, Miller wore bigger shoes to accommodate two pairs of socks. "I still had to look natty," he admits. "I couldn't wear a skull cap. We were in tweed and fifteen sweaters. We were rocking the scarves. We looked like we were Christmas caroling."

Hail or snow, Sterling is open 364 days a year, closing only for Thanksgiving. Every day is a different experience for them and for us. Walking down Northwest Glisan Street and catching the unexpected vapors of fresh-roasting coffee invites a new conversation, and that was the idea behind Sterling Coffee Roasters.

Each day, two single-origin coffees are posted on a handwritten menu. Coffees are identified by country and farm but, more important, by how they taste, summed up by two words that, to Sterling's crew, say it all: Chocolate Skippy, Fruity Pebbles, Sarsaparilla Float, and so on. The idea is to demystify coffee, to eliminate the pretense and intimidation factor. No one should feel uncomfortable— that's the rule. You can geek out over soil composition if you like, or talk about a day at the river—that's the message.

In the end, we're all in on it. We, the fine customers, have been as carefully considered as flavor and temperature control. That's when you realize that craft can be more than product—it's space, it's experience, it's feeling respected.

Parting Thoughts

Portland's coffee landscape is shifting rapidly. Only three years ago, scoring a killer cup of coffee meant a trip to Coffeehouse Northwest, The Albina Press, or Stumptown. When Sterling opened in 2010, microroasting was a little-known field. Now, comparable quality percolates in almost every neighborhood. Even the distinctions between establishments are changing. Observes McGovern, "Before it was quality, now it's geography, and in the near future, when great shops and great coffee are everywhere, it will be personal style and community."

Long gone are the days when Coffeehouse Northwest hung a framed manifesto explaining why no single shots— only doubles—were served. "We were a little pompous," recalls Miller. "We had something to prove, a chip on our shoulders. Now it's more like, 'Drink this, it's awesome . . . and what are your big plans for the weekend?' "

Stumptown has now conquered New York and changed America's coffee conversation. For McGovern and Miller, it remains their inspiration and foil. Stumptown is the living room of coffee culture; Sterling aspires to be the kitchen, the place where everyone gathers for intimacy. It's reaching for something beyond coffee, a trust, an experience, while making sure the conversation is as rewarding as the carefully sourced Ethiopian Yirgacheffe beans.

For Sterling Coffee Roasters, the monolith is no longer relevant. The future is personal.

Most Frequently Asked Question at Sterling Coffee Roasters

"Do you guys sell coffee?"

Epilogue

For months, Sterling waited with fear and trembling for word from their landlord, and now they have it. Two years after launching a street-side gathering space, Sterling lost its lease in spring 2012. But like Sterling's Facebook logo, a figure Miller calls "the perservering man," the show will go on. Says a determined McGovern, "Sterling is a cart. It doesn't look like it, but everything is mobile. We'll relocate some place else if we can maintain the quality; not just the look, not just the coffee, but that sense of specialness, what Sterling is. We won't allow it to be diminished, not even by a small knot."

DA' STERLING BOMBS (ESPRESSO GANACHE–STUFFED CHOCOLATE COOKIES)

Two Tarts Bakery is a kingdom of three-bite cookies and nano-batch ice cream starring artisan neighbors, farmer fruits, and seven kinds of basil grown out front. Owner Elizabeth Beekley goes the distance, literally, running four blocks in Northwest Portland over to Sterling Coffee Roasters for fresh espresso to infuse teeny ice cream sandwiches with a super-roasty intensity. When we challenged her to pull her cookie and coffee obsession into one new idea, Da' Sterling Bombs were born: boisterous sandwich cookies, rugged with dark chips, full of bittersweet goodness, and devoured two at a time with espresso-powered ganache in between. Wow.

Cookies

12 oz/340 g bittersweet chocolate, 60% cocoa, roughly chopped

4 oz/115 g unsalted butter

4 eggs, room temperature

2/3 cup/130 g granulated sugar

2/3 cup/130 g lightly packed brown sugar

1 tsp pure vanilla extract

1/2 cup/60 g unbleached all-purpose flour

1/2 tsp baking powder

12 oz/340 g good-quality dark chocolate chips

Espresso Ganache Filling

8 oz/225 g bittersweet chocolate, 60% cocoa, roughly chopped

1/2 cup plus 2 tbsp/150 ml heavy cream, well chilled

3 tbsp freshly pulled espresso or very strong brewed coffee, cooled

1. TO MAKE THE COOKIES: In the top of a double boiler, melt the chocolate and butter over barely simmering water. As soon as it's melted, stir gently with a spoon and remove from the heat.

2. Meanwhile, combine the eggs, granulated sugar, and brown sugar in the bowl of a stand mixer fitted with the paddle attachment and beat on medium-high speed until thick and pale yellow, about 5 minutes. Reduce the speed to low. Add the vanilla and melted chocolate-butter mixture and mix just until blended.

3. In a medium bowl, combine the flour, baking powder, and chocolate chips. Add to the egg-chocolate mixture, and mix on low, scraping down the sides of the bowl as necessary, until incorporated, 30 seconds. Cover and chill until firm, 2 hours or overnight.

4. Preheat the oven to 325°F/165°C/gas 3. Line a baking sheet with parchment paper.

5. Remove the cookie dough from the refrigerator. Roll or scoop the dough into 1-tsp-size balls, and place them 2 in/5 cm apart on the prepared baking sheet. Bake until barely set and the surface is just starting to crack, 6 to 8 minutes. Transfer to a wire rack and let cool completely before filling.

6. TO MAKE THE ESPRESSO GANACHE FILLING: In the top of a double boiler, melt the chocolate over barely simmering water until smooth. Remove from the heat, then slowly add the cream in a steady stream, whisking continuously. Pour in the espresso and whisk until smooth and glossy.

7. Turn half of the cookies over, and pipe or spoon just under 1 tsp of ganache onto each. Top with remaining halves, tops up, to form a "sandwich" and chill thoroughly to set the ganache. Store in an airtight container in the refrigerator for up to 4 days.

MAKES 2½ DOZEN SANDWICH COOKIES

ELIAS CAIRO & NATE TILDEN
OLYMPIC PROVISIONS

Free-thinking meat geeks rock their own salumi movement.

Behind every movement is a soundtrack, and the anthem of Olympic Provisions' hardcore charcuterie scene is fast, raw, and insanely loud. It's old-school meets extreme meat craft, and dressed in shorts whenever possible. It's repurposing local hogs forty different ways, artfully curing every bit, while spinning vegan straight-edge punk vinyl. It's cutting to the bone, making something happen against the odds. It's blacksmithing your own damn meat hooks and loving every minute.

Every vibrant food city now has butcher shops reveling in ethically raised meat and I-dare-you-to-eat-this bravado. Portland's Olympic Provisions has forged the next step with two handmade meat-curing labs, a salami-of-the-month club, do-it-yourself butcher classes, and a meaty presence on the farmers' market circuit—sometimes seventeen locations in a week. The passion extends to two candle-lit restaurants to riff on the goods and not least, manning a turntable steps away from the sausage line. The no-rules ethos is best expressed on Valentine's Day when OP's "singing salami-gram" service blooms and a couple of guitar-strumming, bearded guys hold out flowery bouquets of stemmed wieners to horrified love interests.

Years ago, John Gardener's short story *The Art of Living* posed a question. How are artists different from ordinary nuts? His chef-philosopher Arnold Geller drew this conclusion: They are "men alive" who never back off. Surely, this is Olympic Provisions in a meaty slice.

Behind the scenes are five owners who operate less like traditional restaurateurs and more like band members howling out original tunes. Never before have you met people more excited about meat, blades, and mig welders. Elias Cairo holds the title of "head salumist" while swingman Nate Tilden functions as manager, egghead, shrink, talent scout, and, not least, chief blow-torch operator and steel cutter. In 2009, with enough volunteers to start a kibbutz, the crew built Oregon's first certified salumeria with a can-do attitude to counterpunch the big zeros in their bank accounts. No cash for a $15,000 incubator? No problem. Cairo bought the parts and knocked it out himself for 800 bucks.

Nate Tilden is wired into the DNA of Portland's food world. His Clyde Common in downtown bundles local sensibility like muscle fibers: a menu of meat-laden locavore

cuisine; full-on communal dining; more ink than a Russian prison; and with customers four deep bellying up to one of America's leading craft bars. For his second act, Olympic Provisions, he designed a witty food-and-wine hideaway in SE Portland's warehouse district while Cairo sat alone, months on end, up to his elbows in pig parts and paperwork, determined to prove that small-scale dreamers could breach territory hogged by the Big Boys: the right to distribute dry-cured meats. That means navigating the resource-sucking, mind-numbing language of the USDA's meat safety certification programs. The name "Hazard Analysis & Critical Control Point Plan" says it all: This is not rock 'n' roll high school.

Passing the grade is just the first hurdle. Big Brother now hawks Cairo's every move at the salumeria, forty hours a week, poking flashlights into grinders, waving thermometers like the Berlin Philharmonic, and swab-testing the walls, floors, and spices without a moment's notice to ensure that we, the good carnivores, stay not just happy but healthy. No sweat. What started as a one-man meat revival has fomented into a booming charcuterie show with fifty employees and small-batch accounts from New York to L.A. Jonah Hill is suddenly Ryan Gosling. Olympic Provisions has become a leading man in America's craft charcuterie story, with A-list artisan butcher status in *Bon Appetit* and *Food & Wine*. In 2011, the group grabbed four Good Food Awards, led by a gasp-worthy pork liver mousse celebrating livers and lard in equal measure. Twittered one fan of the house rillettes following its supermarket debut: "Holy pork. Eat it with a spoon!" Even author Michael Ruhlman, the salami swami himself, calls Cairo's performance outstanding, noting "Olympic Provisions nailed it."

Only What We Love

In Europe, charcuterie refers to the ancient art of preserving meat in transformative expressions of rustic beauty—salamis, sausages, proscuitti, for sure, but also more elaborate specialties like pâtés, terrines, and rillettes. In Portland, it's a way of life, a gastronomy of happy noir from the land of Pink Martini and Gus Van Sant. Here, charcuterie plates are iconic statements. Like bands, tattoos, dark secrets, and dogs, everyone has them. Some restaurants make their stand with curated ham plates or existential arguments over the veracity of local versus the world (a.k.a. New York

Most Surprising Customers at Olympic Provisions

"Vegetarians. We get them all the time. They say, 'I'm a vegetarian and I don't eat meat . . . except your meat.' Vegetarians are among the biggest samplers at our farmers' market booth."

and Italy). But getting in the conversation means breaking the glass salami ceiling in a city where even a neighborhood place boasts its own porchetta di testa made from the meat and skin of a hog's head. Today's player must send forth no less than five options reinforced by architectural precision, fruit pickles, and reimagined mustards in portions large enough to engage a pile of adventurous eaters with less than $20 to burn.

Seattle's Salumi, founded by Armandino "Yes, I'm the Father of Mario" Batali, helped inspire these mad meat tables. Back in the early 2000s, an underground of Portland chefs traveled north to soak in the shoebox atmosphere and smuggle Salumi's salamis back home. As one remembers it, "two jolly old men up front; one long table—always packed; a swoon of polenta; cheap jug wine flowing like the Puget Sound; and mostly Batali, sharing with anyone who would listen the secrets to his extraordinary meats cured in the back." It was charming, contagious, and a vision of what Portland could be: handmade to the max, generous, on its own terms.

Years later, Olympic Provisions organized that energy, opening the way for other sustainable-minded superhero butchers to show how fresh thinking and happy hogs plumped on Oregon peaches and hazelnuts can breed audacious pleasures—with the USDA's blessings. This fresh wave now rises at North Portland's microcharcuterie Chop, where the house muse is the imagined meal of a fat French butcher—full-flavored meats, grabbing the best of everything around. Pâté demon Eric Finley and butcher queen Paula Markus make good on their word: game birds, apples, and chanterelles roam through Chop's jubilant salamis and sandwiches. Meanwhile, at Fino in Fondo two towns over in McMinnville, two young maximalists trained in Umbria

and the trenches of San Francisco's Quince are hand-dicing the back fat of locally raised pigs into beautific, hand-tied Toscanos worthy of sainthood.

Cairo pursues his own salami-without-borders approach, one that honors old-world methods but answers only to the house credo: what we love; local farmers rule; never go cheap; never stop striving for the best. His arsenal moves easily from a rollicking Greek *loukanika* to a double-charged Spanish chorizo. But it also accommodates the sober purity of a French *saucisson d'Arles*, Olympic Provisions' moment of glory, its salami de resistance, with nothing but salt and the flavor of certified organic pigs living high on the hog in straw-lined greenhouses at the esteemed Square Peg Farm, located at the gateway to Oregon's wine country. Cairo says the flavor changes depending on their diet of the moment, noting, "Farmer Chris lets them go crazy in the orchards and gardens." Note to reincarnation hopefuls, the only animals eating better than Portland dogs are Portland pigs.

Even Cairo's "fake" salami, artfully bound in butcher paper, keeps it real—a bittersweet chocolate "link" marbled with cookie crumbs, pistachios, and orange zest; a thick coat of powdered sugar conjures the genuine article. A

playful treat or a sly commentary on Olympic Provisions' business gamble? That craggy, in-your-face natural white mold found on the house salamis encourages aging, personality, and the lick-your-chops flavors that captured Cairo's heart during a three-year Alpine apprenticeship with a wild-game master. Tilden admits their company could increase market share with a more user-friendly look—the standard-issue dusting of fake rice flour favored by industry giants. But where's the fun in that?

SAVORY CHORIZO DOUGHNUTS

It takes a certain diabolical freedom to put spicy chorizo and scallions in addictive little puffs of fried dough, and call it a "doughnut." That's Olympic Provisions. Consider these your perfect party poppers—light, airy, irresistible, and very easy to make. Salumi lord Elias Cairo makes three kinds of Spanish-style chorizos, but here, he favors the cayenne-flecked Navarre because it "packs the most punch." Buy them at the shop or online, or substitute your favorite chorizo.

¼ lb/115 g Spanish-style chorizo, finely diced

2 tbsp olive oil

1 cup/240 ml water

¾ tsp fine sea salt

1 cup/115 g all-purpose flour

3 eggs, at room temperature

¾ cup finely chopped scallions

Pinch of *piment d'Espelette*

4 cups/960 ml vegetable oil, for frying

1. In a small skillet, cook the chorizo in the olive oil over medium heat to release the fat, about 30 seconds to 1 minute.

2. Meanwhile, pour the water into a medium saucepan and add the salt. Place a strainer over the pan of water and strain the chorizo, letting the oil drip into the water. Set the chorizo aside.

3. Bring the water to a boil over medium-high heat. Add the flour all at once, and reduce the heat immediately to low. Using a wooden spoon, stir the dough constantly, until it begins to stick to bottom of the pan, 4 to 5 minutes.

4. Using a spatula, scrape the dough into the bowl of a mixer fitted with a paddle attachment. On low speed, beat in the eggs, one at a time, mixing well. Blend another minute until the dough is smooth and wet. Fold in the chorizo, scallions, and *piment d'Espelette*.

5. In a medium saucepan or deep-fryer, heat the vegetable oil to 385°F/195°C. Form 1-tsp-size balls of dough and carefully drop in the oil, one at a time. Cook a minute or so until very light golden and cooked all the way through. Remove with a slotted spoon to a paper towel–lined plate. Serve warm.

MAKES 4 DOZEN

SALT & STRAW'S MELON AND PROSCIUTTO ICE CREAM

How did thin sheets of Olympic Provisions charcuterie end up rippling through the frozen music of cream and cantaloupe at the flavor-romping Salt & Straw? Long before they redefined ice cream on Portland turf, drew rock-club lines, and grabbed instant national press in 2011, cousins-cum–ice cream dreamers Kim and Tyler Malek had a flash inspiration: to recast fresh melon and prosciutto (Italy's contribution to the sweet-salty pantheon) into local gold with fantastic meatcraft from Portland's slow salumi lords. They cold-called the owners, with no portfolio or even a product, just an idea for a delicious collaboration. OP's response: "Come on over . . . *today*." That's Portland, in a scoop.

1½ cups/340 g cubed ripe cantaloupe

1 cup/235 ml whole milk

2 cups/475 ml heavy cream

3 egg yolks

¾ cup/150 g granulated sugar

Dash of salt

¼ cup/60 ml corn syrup

Juice from ½ lemon

2 oz/55 g prosciutto or coppa salami, sliced paper-thin

1. In a blender, puree the cantaloupe until smooth. Scrape into a medium saucepan and stir in the milk. Cook over medium heat, stirring occasionally, until the mixture just begins to boil. Immediately remove from the heat and let sit for 20 minutes. Transfer the mixture back to the blender and puree another minute or so.

2. Line a strainer with cheesecloth and set over a bowl. Pour in the puree. Using a rubber spatula, scrape and press the melon to help the milk pass through the cheesecloth. Discard the cheesecloth and melon fibers.

3. Return the strained mixture to the saucepan, and stir in the cream. Cook over medium heat, stirring frequently, until the mixture reaches 155°F/68°C on a thermometer, about 5 minutes. Remove from the heat.

4. In a large bowl, combine the egg yolks, sugar, and salt, whisking vigorously about 30 seconds. Slowly pour ½ cup/120 ml of the warm cream mixture into the yolk mixture, whisking constantly. Add another ½ cup/120 ml, whisking to combine. Then, pour the yolk mixture into the saucepan, stirring to combine with any remaining cream mixture. Whisk in the corn syrup and lemon juice. Cook over medium heat to 165°F/74°C, stirring constantly and being careful not to boil (or the eggs will scramble). Pour into a medium bowl, cover the surface with plastic wrap, and refrigerate at least 8 hours.

5. Pour the mixture into an ice cream maker and churn according to the manufacturer's directions. When the ice cream reaches a thick, soft-serve consistency, turn off the machine. Immediately ladle ¼ cup/60 ml of the ice cream into a 1-qt/960-ml metal or plastic container. Add a single layer of prosciutto or coppa, then ladle another ¼ cup/60 ml of ice cream over the meat. Continue layering, finishing with a final layer of ice cream. Cover and freeze for at least 12 hours before serving.

MAKES 1 QT/960 ML

KURT HUFFMAN

CHEFSTABLE + GRUNER + ST. JACK + WAFU + OVEN & SHAKER + OX

A one-man restaurant company banks on crazy idealists.

Portland's debut as the "announcement city" for nominations leading up to the James Beard Foundation Awards in New York arrived on a brisk and sunny March afternoon. But inside the Oregon Culinary Institute, the air was tighter than the stock market floor during President Obama's "let's get tough on Wall Street" speech. Soon, names of The Chosen would ring out as ballot-worthy finalists in the Oscars of the food world. Careers would surge; egos teeter.

Whims, Ricker, and Rucker made the final cut. So did Gruner's Christopher Israel, a mad man of Mitteleuropa cooking in a downtown jewel box of his own design. People rip into Gruner's salt-crusted pretzel bread and brioche donuts like lions eating prey; even the menu fonts are food for obsession. A year ago, an anti-schnitzel brigade wondered if even Israel could make magic out of the lumpen and the uncool. The answer came swiftly as diners, discerning critics, and not least, Beard's secret cabal of judges, climbed Gruner's alps and found otherworldly vistas: thin-cut radishes displayed like Indian mandalas; beet-hued deviled eggs glowing like ruby slippers; cider-poached calves' liver tender enough to make grown men weep.

GQ magazine called Gruner one of America's best newcomers, solidifying the rise of its creative business arm— ChefStable, a one-man restaurant company run by a cherubic egghead named Kurt Huffman. ChefStable is the Krazy Glue behind a string of unlikely hits, including Ricker's Ping in Chinatown, which follows only its guts and bones and isn't afraid to park either one inside a bun.

Two months later, Ricker won Best Chef Northwest, Rucker bagged Rising Star, and Portland's food revolution officially moved out of the underground.

Change is coming. At an accelerated pace, from diverse sources, and with predictable regularity, national recognition is being slathered on the mighty gastropolis that is Portland, Oregon. The food world has fallen in love with this whacky, interconnected, rule-bending, bottle-aging, "food brother," live-to-eat, head-cheese-con-feet food culture. No one captures the moment better than *Saveur* editor James Oseland in late 2011, "Portland, Ore., has some of the best food not only in this country, but anywhere in the world. From the hundreds of fantastic food trucks to the city's high-end dining of Paley's Place and Beast, gastronomically speaking, the city completely rocks. This is where artisanal

farm-to-table meets global food meets really great, smart American culinary ingenuity. It's just awesome."

Who would have guessed that the food elite would delight in the willfully anti-elite? Who would have thought in the flamboyant days of Louie XIV that someday a former loading dock in the middle of a deserted warehouse district and someone's daydream would serve food fit for a king? Or that the Beaver State would infiltrate New York's state of mind?

It makes sense to food festival mastermind Mike Thelin, who brings chefs from the growing axis of Portland, Austin, and New York under one experimental tent: "New York is the Mecca, but the entire conversation is shifting. Portland is leading that swing to evangelical sourcing and indifference to pedigree. The big question in food right now is simply, 'Is it good?' It's shaking up a system that has been in place for many years."

Not too long ago, Stumptown's big bean hunter Duane Sorenson U-Hauled across the country and rewired Gotham with what he calls "the most bitchingest coffees in the world." Even New Yorkers didn't argue. Now Matt Lightner, lured to the big city, has put found berries and forgotten roots in the center of his new restaurant Atera, and it's wilder than anything in TriBeca. Meanwhile, the Big Apple is now the Big Fish Sauce Wings with Andy Ricker's Pok Pok encursion in 2012. As one NYC food blog playfully pondered: "Is New York About to Become New Portland?"

What does it all mean? How will Portland respond to the attention, the steady diet of tweets from food dignitaries? Nearly every high-profile cook is fielding calls, franchise offers, or cookbook deals. Will Portland be devoured by the taste of celebrity like Seattle's grunge scene or evolve into a street-smart Silicon Valley for food?

Fighters, Scrappers, Crazy Idealists

One man thinks he has the answer. When indie entrepreneur Kurt Huffman surveys the landscape, he sees a Wild West rumbling with iconoclastic models and new prospects. "Think about schools of thought in philosophy or art or food. Interesting things happen in isolated geographic locations over short periods of time—Bocuse in Lyon in the '70s; avant garde cooking coming out of a small area in Spain. In Portland, new models keep emerging,

things you don't see elsewhere. Andy Ricker could take Pok Pok to fifty cities. It would be a nightmare for him, but he could do it. Bunk Sandwiches could go anywhere. Nong's Khao Mon Gai? A food truck perfecting one dish. I've never seen anyone with a more enthusiastic following. Fifteen years ago, no one thought about great things happening in parking lots. Portland cooks come up with ideas that would never come out of corporate kitchens."

Huffman's point hits home as booming enterprises around the city recraft mainstream ideas. It's a rare place indeed where you can get a Bacon Maple Bar and a new bride. But Voodoo Doughnuts, launched in 2003 in a sketchy stretch of downtown, slaps Krispy Kreme upside its head with ordained wedding vows and doughnut rings to match dozens of nonconformist wonders conjured with pure adolescent glee. Voodoo once glazed a house special in Nyquil until health officials ordered an end to that delicacy. But you can still find an "Old Dirty Bastard" or a stun-faced, chocolate-coated donut doll stabbed with a pretzel stick and spurting red-jelly "blood." Even Anthony Bourdain fell under the spell. A perpetual line snakes out of doors that never close, and revenues (at three locations) are looking anything but fried: an estimated 7 million in 2011.

Nearby, another new empire grows: Little Big Burger. If Ray Kroc went to the Rhode Island School of Design, history may have looked like this: fast and fun, eco-minded, lit up with mind-bending murals, serving genuine food, a swagger of truffle fries for less than three clams, and instead of cartoon mascots, canned beer—nearly two dozens brands stacked on shelves as though posing for a Warhol painting.

Huffman is riding this energy, harnessing new talent and reinvigorating the old guard, while seeding the ground for the next phase of this food frontier. He's not leading the war on corporate food culture—just organizing it. In 2009, as napkin-wringing over the economy took a bite out of ambition, restaurant openings in Portland became as rare as happy news from Afghanistan. Huffman swooped in like a superhero and bam, eight places ignited, with more on the way.

ChefStable handpicks culinary dreamers and lets them do what they do best while Huffman dogs the books and boring details that chefs notoriously mangle, sharing ownership and profits at varying percentages. While Huffman's warriors divine pig parts, he juggles hats as contractor,

tough-guy lease negotiator, systems guru, HR department, and legal eagle. Sometimes he invests his own money, but often, chefs are enlisted to find willing investors and help with construction, so everyone is invested.

ChefStable's charm bracelet now includes Cathy Whims' new Oven & Shaker, a playful pizzeria with serious cocktails. At the ramen bistro Wafu, handrolls are packaged with roasted crab, lamb tongue gets a brazen dunk in gin-spiked ponzu, and cocktails arrive with hand-carved ice. Ox plows its own turf. Portland-meets-Argentina, in a blaze of gonzo gaucho eating from rising stars Greg and Gabrielle Quiñónez Denton. This is food as primal scream. Octopus and freshly stuffed chorizos blister before your eyes on a state-of-the-art, hand-cranked wooden spit. Less than thirty days after opening, Ox jumped straight onto *Food & Wine*'s list of best new pit masters—a triumph of the grill, indeed.

As the accolades pile up, ChefStable's formula seems to be no formula at all: build your own blueprints; invest in point of view, not the easy sells; keep it fun and afford-able. The sky is the limit as long as the entree costs under $20. That's the whole calculation right there; the secret to Portland's success. Everyone gets the good stuff; the bike messenger is asking the same question as the mayor: "Have you been to St. Jack yet?"

Call it the survival of the passionate. Portland drives on people believing they can make something happen, for almost nothing. In the end, there's no other way to succeed here; no money to burn. Banks aren't lending it. Diners don't have it. That forces everyone to think differently.

Huffman believes something important is happening in The City of Roses, and he's gambling his future on it. "I don't know how long it will stay, but I want to be part of it. Lack of money somehow doesn't burden how dynamic things are here. A whole new generation is figuring out how to do it themselves. I recently ate at Next, the conceptual Thai restaurant in Chicago. Those guys are working on a level we will never have. Eight chefs standing around with tweezers, one chef per bowl putting on micro-greens! It was great. But I come from Portland. Two hundred dollars for a meal? For the same money, I could get a back massage and as much as I want to drink. We're fighters, scrappers. Portland cultivates crazy idealists. You know what? If you mix crazy with talent, something really good is going to happen."

THE MIGHTY
GASTROPOLIS COCKTAIL

As we end this journey, a toast is in order: a mighty thanks to the great gastrobashers and plucky pioneers who inspired this book and conspired to build America's great new food city. In scouring this land of great drinking, we landed on one cocktail that says it all: simple, finely tuned, amazing, made of gin with muddled strawberries and pickled rhubarb. In creating the formula, Gruner's Christopher Israel, an icon of Portland dining, blended the essence of Portland's drink scene: local spirits (Aviation Gin), local fruit (Oregon's world-class strawberries), a taste of the unexpected (Campari-like Aperol) and, of course, a pickle project (pickled rhubarb garnish). Cheers.

3¼ cups/840 ml water

1½ cups/300 g sugar

¾ cup/180 ml Riesling wine vinegar or other sweet vinegar

2 lb/910 g (6 to 8 stalks) rhubarb, ends trimmed

12 sweet ripe strawberries

9 oz/265 ml Aviation or other favorite gin

3 oz/90 ml Aperol

10 ice cubes

1. In a small saucepan, combine ¼ cup/60 ml of the water, ½ cup/100 g of the sugar and the vinegar over medium heat until just boiling, stirring to dissolve the sugar. Meanwhile, cut two of the rhubarb stalks in half crosswise, into ½-in/12-mm pieces. Place the rhubarb in a nonreactive bowl and cover with the hot vinegar mixture. Cover the bowl with plastic wrap and let sit for an hour. (You can also pickle the rhubarb 2 weeks in advance, refrigerated and stored in its liquid).

2. Chop the remaining rhubarb into 1-in/2.5-cm chunks. Place in a medium saucepan, stir in remaining sugar and water, and bring to a boil over medium-high heat. Reduce to a simmer, partially cover the pan, and cook, stirring occasionally, for about 15 minutes. Cool 20 minutes in the pan, then strain the rhubarb syrup through a fine-mesh sieve or strainer, pushing down on the fruit to release the juices. Return the syrup to the pot and reduce over high heat, stirring, for about 10 minutes.

3. Place the strawberries in a bowl and using a muddler or potato masher, smash the fruit into a smooth purée. (If the strawberries are very tart, you can add a spoonful of sugar.) Skewer three pieces of pickled rhubarb onto each of six wooden sewers.

4. Place half of the strawberries in a cocktail shaker with 1½ oz/45 ml of the rhubarb syrup, 4½ oz/135 ml of gin, 1½ oz/45 ml of Aperol, and 5 ice cubes. Shake vigorously until chilled. Strain into three small tumblers, and garnish each with the skewered rhubarb. Repeat to make three additional drinks and serve.

NOTE: There will be leftover rhubarb syrup, enough to use for more cocktails or add to sparkling water for homemade soda.

MAKES 6 DRINKS

INDEX

C

D